CHASING THE CHECKERED FLAG

Kay Presto

ISBN: 1535597542
ISBN 13: 9781535597548
Library of Congress Control Number: 2016912816
Createspace Independent Publishing Platform
North Charleston, South Carolina
Cover Borg-Warner Trophy Photo - Courtesy of BorgWarner
Cover Art 2016 by Hector Cademartori
Cover Design 2016 by Flori Cademartori

ACKNOWLEDGMENTS

For their information and invaluable help, I thank:

My loving and supportive family, Deb, Rich, Lee, Tony and all, Adams Motorsports Park in California, Chris and Karen Koch, Terry Nash, Seth Nash, Kasey Nash, Dwight Davis, Cary Agajanian, Chuck Sihler, Esteban M. Danna, U. S. Navy Department of Sea, Air, and Land (SEALs), Paula Emick, Dr. Margaret Albertson, C.H.AI.R.S., and the young boys and girls who eagerly shared their love of go-karting with me.

TABLE OF CONTENTS

Chapter One	1
Chapter Two	16
Chapter Three	21
Chapter Four	29
Chapter Five	35
Chapter Six	48
Chapter Seven	59
Chapter Eight	65
Chapter Nine	78
Chapter Ten	90
Chapter Eleven	97
Chapter Twelve	107
Chapter Thirteen	112
Chapter Fourteen	123
Chapter Fifteen	128
Chapter Sixteen	135
About the Author	143

FOREWORD

The story of a young go-karter, Ryan, and his dream of winning a championship and moving to the upper echelons of motorsports is something that I can relate unequivocally to. My own motorsport journey started in a very similar way in a virtually unknown town in Northern California. Through an incredible amount of hard work by my entire family, seven years spent racing overseas, countless moments of elation and even more moments of mind-numbing heartbreak, we were able to make history by winning the 100th Running of the Indianapolis 500.

Ryan's growing relationship with his father, the obstacles that he has to overcome and the continual pursuit of improvement are all things that motorsport has given me. My father is my hero for a lot of things in life, but most specifically for the one piece of advice that he gave me when I was ten years old. "You can do absolutely anything that you want if you work hard enough for it. Don't let anyone ever tell you otherwise." This approach was something that not only impacted my racing career, but also changed my perspective of the world and what was possible.

One does not to have to look very hard to see the multiple examples of hard-work, fearlessness, loyalty and respect, all conveyed in a beautiful way in different applications and relationships throughout this book. Ryan's journey spoke to me as an adult, a young go-karter, and an Indianapolis 500 winner, and I sincerely hope that it does the same for you.

— Alexander Rossi, Winner of the 100th Running of the Indianapolis 500, 2016

CHAPTER ONE

V-R-O-O-M-M!!!

Ryan Edwards' go-kart screamed around the track at speeds of 80 miles an hour, the wind whipping rapidly over his helmet. His body was quivering with excitement. The big weekend race was approaching, and this was the last day of practice. He never felt more ready in his life!

The course at Atlas Motorsports Park is a challenging three-quarter-mile track. Soaring in and out over the asphalt surface among the other racers, he maneuvered his way through another curve, gunning his kart around that difficult section with ease, then powering into the final 700-foot long straight.

On the slight banking at that track, his kart had handled the high speeds better than ever.

That solid *w-h-i-n-e* of Ryan's 125cc engine was music to his ears! With his heart pounding from the speed, he quickly steered his kart over the rumble strips into the next turn, saving precious driving seconds. Ryan knew that every time he took the shortest line through a curve, he could work his way up to the front and beat out the other drivers on race day. His kart was performing perfectly. He definitely owned the world -- now!

It was at a track like this that Indianapolis 500 winner Ryan Hunter-Reay and other IndyCar race drivers had probably learned *their* go-kart racing skills! From Hunter-Reay's bio, Ryan knew that Hunter-Reay had won nine World Karting Association/FIA National Series go-karting championships and three Grand National titles! He had worked his way up in racing to eventually win the IndyCar Series championship in 2012, and the famed Indianapolis 500 race in 2014. "If Hunter-Reay could get started on *all that* through go-karting," Ryan said to himself as he drove, "my own go-kart racing could certainly help *me* get to race at Indianapolis some day!"

Suddenly, another kart roared by him, just missing him by a scant quarter-inch! Ryan snapped his steering wheel to the right just in time, swerving out of the way, so his kart wasn't hit! Then he saw who it was – his racing enemy, for sure!

It was Kyle Sampson, the bully in his go-kart series! Kyle never completely broke the rules, so he couldn't be suspended, but he was wickedly good at bending them as far as he could.

"You better watch your back, Kyle," Ryan shouted inside his helmet, waving his fist. "I'll get you yet!" He drove his kart swiftly up the slight banking, and cranked it into a slight downward turn to the right. He shot it down onto the final long straight, slowed, steered his kart off the track, came to a stop, and switched off the engine.

A tall man standing by his pit held out his stopwatch. It was his dad.

"Did you see that crazy stunt Kyle just pulled?" Ryan yelled. Ripping off his racing gloves, he threw them to the ground. "I ought to beat him to a pulp!" he yelled again, as he angrily whipped off his helmet.

"Yep, I saw it, and it was nuts," said his dad. "I also saw the great evasive maneuver you made when he tried to take you out, Ryan. Great job of driving out there." In a lower voice, he said, "Just ignore Kyle, he's just a nasty kid who doesn't know any better."

Once Ryan settled down his anger, his dad showed him his lap times. "Your fastest times yet!" he said, with a grin. "You've certainly improved even more since last week!"

"Yahoo!" Ryan yelled, pumping his fist in the air. "That's great news, Dad! If I keep up that speed, I can probably beat all the other guys this weekend."

At 12 years of age, Ryan's bedroom shelves were already dotted with small trophies, plaques, coins, and other racing mementoes of his on-track go-karting achievements.

But there was one important item missing. He hadn't won it yet.

It was the famous Jason Waldron trophy, named after one of the greatest go-kart racers of all time.

Ryan yahoo'd again. He'd already picked out the perfect location for that trophy, and had vowed that it would be *his* by the end of the season.

Better yet, he had a second place cleared on his shelf. That special spot was for the other, far-greater trophy – *the Baby Borg*. Every race driver who wins the historic Indianapolis 500-mile race in Indiana has his name and face sculpted on that historic Borg-Warner trophy. Each driver also gets their own smaller trophy to keep, called the Baby Borg. With his eye on the far future, Ryan was working hard to learn how to be a great race driver, so he could earn his own Baby Borg someday.

Later that night, he was hard at work in his garage, loud music blaring from his radio. He was dead-set on winning that weekend. His go-kart had to be in perfect shape.

"How's that machine of yours coming along?"

He looked up. It was his dad. They had worked together on his karts since Ryan was eight, when he began racing in the Cadet Corps division of the South-Cal Karters Club.

"It's doing great. I think it'll run perfectly on Saturday."

Saturday was the big monthly race. Ryan's heart pounded hard every time he thought of winning that Main! There were several other drivers that usually ran quicker than he did, so it would be one tough contest! His last practice had been faster than their times, but again, there was Kyle Sampson, who seemed to be faster and better than all the others – every single week!

Sampson was the one Ryan wanted to beat the most. In last month's Main, he had battled tight on Kyle's tail over most the course, and came in a close second to him – a scant 0.23 seconds behind. "This time," muttered Ryan under his breath, "I'm going to win that final."

He smacked his fist down hard on the workbench. "My go-kart's as powerful as Kyle's, Dad, and I know I'm just as good a racer as he is."

"No doubt in *my* mind, son. You can do it."

"You bet," Ryan shot back. "Between you and me, we'll be the best team at the track this weekend. I'll put my kart *wherever I have to* on that track to *win*."

"Sounds great to me. Now if you'll turn off that loud noise you call music, and get on some great *New York Sound*, I'll help you finish up."

It was a constant joke between them. Ryan loved rock and heavy metal, but his dad liked the quiet *New York Sound,* which hardly ever got airplay anymore, except on the local 5000-watt station in town. Clicking their workshop radio over to that station, Ryan slipped on the earbuds to his MP3, for his own favorite music. Now -- they were ready to get busy.

For the next hour, they worked intensely, checking every bolt, nut, and vital engine wire. They checked the engine to see if the wire clips were fastened correctly on their particular bolts. They also checked the entire chassis.

As they moved from one job to another, Ryan's dog snoozed in his dog bed under the nearby bench. He was the newest member of the family. For a minute, Ryan thought back to how he got his great new pet...

The weekend before, there was a rat-a-tat-tat on the kitchen door. It was Uncle John, loud and boisterous, as usual, not like Ryan's dad, who was quiet and methodical.

"Hey, Ryan, how's everything going today? You ready for a surprise?"

He gave a wink to Ryan's dad. They'd been planning this for a while.

A surprise? Ryan wasn't quite sure what he meant.

"Well, are you or aren't you?" Uncle John teased.

"Well, yeah, I guess so. Whatta ya have in mind?"

"Had your breakfast?"

"Yep."

"Okay, then hop in my truck. We're going for a ride."

Going anywhere with Uncle John was always fun. Ryan grabbed his jacket, dashed out the door, and climbed into Uncle John's sturdy work truck. Moving fast through the busy streets of the city, Ryan couldn't figure out where they were headed. As they drove, his uncle had a happy grin on his face. But then, of course, he always did.

"You gonna tell me where we're goin'?"

"Nope."

"Well, can you give me some kind of clue?"

"Nope."

Soon they were rolling out toward a different part of town. Uncle John still didn't say another word.

Figuring he'd soon find out, Ryan leaned back to enjoy the ride. Finally, they pulled up in front of a building. Above the door were large letters, "TOWNSHIP PET SHELTER."

What are we gonna do here? Ryan wondered. As a contractor, did Uncle John have some work to do inside?

"Okay, hop out," said his uncle.

"You bet," said Ryan. At least now he might find out the mystery. As they entered the shelter, they heard loud barking, yipping, and cat yowls bouncing off the cement shelter walls, like an explosion of sound inside a cave.

"So why are we *here?*" Ryan questioned.

"Well, you lost your dog Skeeter to old age last year." Ryan had Skeeter since he was a baby.

"Yeah, I sure do miss him."

"Thought so. Your dad and I figured it was time you got another dog."

"Another dog for me? Sweet!"

He turned toward the cages. "Wow! Wonder where all these dogs came from?"

"From lots of places," Uncle John answered. "Some from homes where people had to move and couldn't keep their pets, others brought in as strays. Let's take a look and see if you can find another Skeeter."

As they walked along the cages, Ryan spotted a familiar face -- Maria Martinez, his neighbor across the street.

"What're *you* doin' here?"

"I volunteer here. And why are you here, Ryan?"

"You remember Uncle John. He brought me to pick out another dog."

"That's great!" A smile spread across her face. "We have a couple here I think you'll really like."

They headed down the long line of cages. "Here's one of 'em."

Ryan looked where she was pointing.

On the front of the cage, a card read: "Mini Doberman Pinscher. Male, two years old. Brought in as a stray from a field." Getting down on his knees, Ryan spoke to the dog.

"Hi, fella. Sounds like you've had a rough time." The Pinscher put his front paws on the bars of the cage and barked back at Ryan. Ryan liked the dog's peppiness, but inside the next cage, he heard sharp barking, and sounds of lots of fast-moving action. That card read: "West Highland Terrier. One-year-old male. Found as a stray beside a gas station."

Moving quickly to that cage, Ryan crouched down to see that frisky animal. The Westie jumped up, locked his diamond-shaped brown eyes on Ryan, loudly barking and yipping as if he wanted to be taken home right then. This dog had spunk and spirit, just like Ryan. The more Ryan talked to him, the more the Westie jumped up and down.

Ryan laughed. "This spunky little guy wants to go home with me."

Maria nodded. "He really likes you, Ryan. We can write up all his papers right away. We'll figure out the cost for you."

"What say we make those arrangements?" said his uncle.

When Maria showed him the amount to pay, Ryan's heart sank. "I really like this dog, but – it costs more than I have," he mumbled. "I've put most of my money into my kart."

"That's my surprise," said Uncle John. "I'll pay for everything -- the vaccination, neutering, and even for an I.D. microchip under his skin, in case he ever wanders off."

"Wow! That's terrific!" Ryan shouted, breaking into a grin.

At the counter, Maria helped with the arrangements.

"This little fella has been one of our favorites," said the counter clerk. "Westies are such prized dogs, we hardly ever get one of these in here." Finishing the paperwork, she slid it across the counter to be signed. "We're glad he's found a good home. You can pick him up on Wednesday."

Heading toward home, talk bounced around the truck about dog names.

"Tripper's a good name for a dog," said Uncle John.

"Nah," said Ryan, laughing. "That sounds like he'd be tripping all over himself."

"Then how about Boomer?"

"That name really sucks! I'd never name a dog of mine Boomer!" It got very quiet inside the truck. They were wracking their brains about names.

"I got it!" Ryan suddenly yelled. "I'm going to call him -- 'Sparkplug.'"

They looked at each other. Seemed like a perfect fit. "Sparkplug" it was.

Once they were back home, he gave his uncle a high-five of thanks.

"No problem, Ryan. You have yourself a neat pet."

In the kitchen, his mom and dad were waiting. "Well, did you find a new dog?"

"Got a winner -- a Highland Westie. I think he's pretty special." Rushing toward the kitchen door, he gave his uncle another solid high-five as he was leaving.

As the sound of his uncle's truck faded off into the distance, his dad put his arm around Ryan's shoulder. "Okay, young man, let's find out what kind of dog you got yourself."

Ryan laughed. "At the pound, they called him 'pugnacious.' What the heck does that mean?" Taking the stairs two at a time, he and his dad went up to Ryan's room. Grabbing his iPad, Ryan Googled for "pugnacious." The screen read: "Pugnacity – Likes to fight when angry."

Google also said that Westies make good watch-dogs.

"Boy, Dad, I can hardly wait to get him! By the way, I'm going to call him 'Sparkplug.'"

Wednesday found them headed for the shelter. Ryan was so anxious to get there he kept squirming in his seat. On the ride home, his new dog had curled right up in his lap, as if he'd belonged there all the time. And now -- as Ryan and his dad worked in the garage, Sparkplug slept peacefully.

"Be sure to check those wire clips on each wheel again, so nothing will fall off during the race."

"Okay, Dad." Everything had to be perfect to make it through technical inspection.

Suddenly, Sparkplug's short ears shot up. He let out a sinister growl.

"What is it, Sparkplug? Whatta you hear?" A frown creased Ryan's forehead. He took a quick glance out into the yard, then leaned back in. "Nothing goin' on out there, Dad." They went back to work on the kart.

Sparkplug growled again, jumping up in his dog bed, snarling and whoofing toward the garage door.

This time, Ryan's dad went outside, checking all the way round the garage. "Nothing out there that I could see," he said, coming back in. "Just a few bushes moving in the breeze."

Ryan leaned down to pet Sparkplug. "It's his first week in our place," he said. "He probably got spooked by some bushes blowing, or a passing car."

"Yeah, you're probably right."

Back at the kart, they finished one final and very important job – cleaning and lubricating the chain that links the wheels to that powerful engine. Their kart was now ready to take on all comers!

"Hey, guys, dinnertime! Come on in before the food's cold." It was Mom, yelling from the kitchen door.

"Okay, son, let's wrap it up and see what's on the menu tonight. Your mom promised us a special surprise."

Rubbing his greasy hands on his jeans, Ryan bolted out the garage door. "First one in the house gets seconds on dessert!" he yelled, running toward the kitchen.

"No fair!" his dad yelled to the disappearing Ryan. "I have to put away the last of these tools!" Hopping out of his dog bed, Sparkplug scurried out quickly too. But he stopped abruptly outside the garage door and began to bark – a loud angry bark, toward the far corner of the garage. Then he crouched down, letting out a low, sinister growl in that direction.

"What is it, boy?" Ryan said, rushing back to pet him. He could tell Sparkplug was nervous. The dog's small body was quivering under his hand, but they could not find anything strange outside.

"Probably take him a little time to get used to all our neighborhood noises," Ryan said. Scooping up the dog, he and his dad continued toward the house. Sparkplug still growled and huffed, even as they stepped inside. Plopping him under the kitchen table, Ryan scolded him.

"There!" he said. "That should be a more peaceful place for you."

After his doggy dinner, Sparkplug finally did calm down.

Over their chicken and fries, Ryan and his dad talked about the competition.

"Of course, Kyle will be strong; he always is," Ryan said.

"And don't forget – there's a new competitor arriving at our circuit very soon," his dad reminded him.

"That's right, the champion from San Gorgonio County."

"What's his name? Joe Yoshida? I hear he's a pretty tough guy to beat."

"Yep, he has quite the reputation, but I can still beat him, too."

"Keep up that confidence, and you can beat them all."

As his mother cleared the table, Ryan leaned back in his chair. Closing his eyes, he had a vision of himself in Saturday's Victory Circle.

"Here's the surprise I promised you," his mom announced.

Ryan opened his eyes. There sat a plate of freshly-baked cobbler, with the hot and juicy aroma of peaches -- picked from their backyard tree that afternoon. And it was topped with vanilla ice cream! His absolute favorite!

But just as he took his first bite, Sparkplug was at it again, ears straight up on alert. This time, he was up on his hind legs, barking loudly out the low kitchen window. Reaching down, Ryan tried to calm him, but Sparkplug would have none of it! He kept barking and snarling by the window.

"I guess it's going to take a while for him to get used to *everything* around here," Ryan said. He picked Sparkplug up and plopped him in his lap.

"Now calm down, you feisty dog, and let me enjoy my cobbler!" With a few angry grumbles, Sparkplug finally settled down.

After dinner, Ryan and his dad headed back to the garage. They had to make one final check on his Rotax-engined kart. Ryan had Sparkplug carefully tucked under his arm. As they approached the garage, the dog alerted again, making low growling noises.

Putting him down onto his bed inside the garage, Ryan wagged his finger at the Westie. "That's enough! No more noise from you!"

Reluctantly, the dog quieted down.

CHAPTER TWO

South-Cal was club racing, but Ryan's dream was not just to win local championships. He planned to move up to Regional, National, and International competition. At a very early age, he had set his eventual goal -- to race, and *win* – in the Indianapolis 500!

He'd worked hard to get to this club level. Mowed endless lawns, raked leaves, did errands and small painting jobs for neighbors -- any job he could find. Under his mom's constant urging, he reluctantly kept his room clean. In school, his courses were tough – especially Algebra -- but he struggled to keep his grades up.

When Ryan began racing as a youngster, his dad noticed he had natural talent. Still, he hired a professional coach for him for a few sessions.

Happy behind the wheel, Ryan had soaked up all that training – how to accelerate, yet hold the proper speed -- how to pass another racer "clean," how to stick the nose of his kart into a corner and take the spot away from his competitor without making contact.

But karting had proved to be expensive. Although she loved being a homemaker, his mom took a part-time job as a bookkeeper. His dad, retired from the Navy, had a consulting business.

Inside the garage, the two went over the kart one more time. Ryan had cleaned it up thoroughly after his practice. It looked like new. He was extremely proud of the color scheme he'd chosen. His favorite – red, white, and blue. The design on his race helmet matched his kart. It also had an American flag painted on the top, with stars on each side. Every time he looked at that flag, his heart swelled with pride for his dad. He'd served in the military, and been severely wounded. He had a permanent limp, and had received a Silver Star, but would never talk about it.

Ryan knew about the Silver Star. It always hung on the wall by his dad's dresser. Ryan often wished he'd discuss it. He just never wanted to ask.

Like a professional race team, the two of them went over their checklist. Finally, each item was marked off. Time to lock up the garage. When they opened the garage door to leave, Sparkplug flew off his dog bed, barking loudly -- again -- at something outside! Once more, Ryan caught him and calmed him down, stroking his short fur as the dog kept muttering low angry growls. As they walked toward the house, neither Ryan nor his dad noticed the person lurking nearby.

Just as they reached the house, there was a loud crash -- beside the garage! Startled, they ran to see what happened! Leaping out of Ryan's arms, Sparkplug flew on ahead, running toward something.

As they approached, they spotted a person lying there in the glow of the garage light, next to a small stool on the ground. It was Timmy, their next-door neighbor! Sparkplug was busy licking Timmy's face. Trying to get up, Timmy looked extremely embarrassed.

"Are you hurt?" Mr. Edwards asked with concern. He shooed Sparkplug away.

"No."

Carefully, Ryan and his dad picked Timmy up. "What were you doing by our garage?" Ryan asked.

"The inside light was on and I-I-I just climbed up on a stool to see your go-kart through the window," Timmy stammered. Using his sleeve, he wiped his face, still wet where Sparkplug had licked him.

"Why would you do *that*?"

"Cuz my dad wants to get me a Cadet kart, and I wanted to see yours. I know it's even faster than a Cadet."

"Timmy, you don't have to sneak around," Ryan said, fighting to hold back a chuckle. He knew Timmy was not a bad kid. He was just a curious, and slightly mischievous, nine-year-old. "If I'm working on my kart and have time to talk, you can come in our garage and see me anytime."

Timmy's eyes grew wide. "You're not mad at me for sneakin' around?"

Ryan laughed. "Nah. We know you didn't mean anything bad. Heck, you can even come to the track with us sometimes."

"Gee, that'd be lots of fun!" Timmy gushed. "I'll go tell my dad!"

"Tell him to come over after this weekend, and we'll be glad to answer any questions he needs to ask."

"I sure will!" said Timmy, grabbing his stool and running off eagerly toward his house. "I might bring my grampa, too," he yelled over his shoulder. "And I really like your new dog," he yelled, as an afterthought.

Chuckling to themselves, Ryan and his dad headed toward the house. "I'm sure relieved that it was just Timmy, and he wasn't hurt," said Ryan.

"Me, too," added his dad. "And now we know that's probably what kept spooking Sparkplug earlier this evening."

"I guess you're right," said Ryan. But then he stopped -- with a sudden thought.

"Dad, if Sparkplug had been growling and barking because Timmy was outside, why would he end up licking his face when he fell?"

Neither one of them could come up with an answer for that. And neither one of them had noticed a shadowy figure quietly slip away from the *other* side of the garage.

As they both settled down to sleep that night, they had no suspicions that even *more puzzling things would show up in the weeks ahead...*

CHAPTER THREE

Saturday dawned bright and clear, with just a slight breeze. Perfect racing weather. Ryan and his dad carefully loaded up their truck. Sparkplug trotted eagerly toward Ryan's feet. Lifting him up, he took him back inside the house. "Sorry, fella," he said. "No dogs allowed at the track. You'll have to stay home with Mom."

When they arrived at Atlas, the place was already abuzz with activity. Trucks and trailers were pulling in from everywhere. Racing banners on the track fences were whipping in the breeze. Karts were being unloaded, announcements blared from the speakers overhead on the announcing tower. There were people everywhere. Many had slept in a motorhome overnight to get a head start.

The bleachers were rapidly filling with family members who came to watch the racing. There was constant chatter all around. Engines were being switched on and off, for last-minute testing. The air was electric. Every race team there could feel it. They were all there to compete – and to win!

Except, of course, Ernie Farlow. He and his dad showed up every time, but Ernie always just ran in the middle of the pack, never improving his position.

One day Ryan could stand it no longer. He had to ask. "Hey, Ernie, why is it that you never run closer to the front? You have a pretty decent kart."

Ernie smiled at the question. "That's easy. I don't come here to compete; I race go-karts just to race."

That answer was puzzling to Ryan, whose competitive spirit burned so deep within his veins. "It's just a hobby for me," Ernie said. "I enjoy being out here with everyone on the weekends. Just doing that is my fun." Although that was tough for Ryan to understand, Ernie's big smile explained it all. Like he said, he was just -- having fun.

Carefully, Ryan and his dad unloaded their kart, already mounted on its' kart stand. Wheeling it over to tech inspection, they heard a familiar voice behind them. It was Kyle Sampson.

"I see you brought your old scumbucket to race again today," he sneered. Ryan's stomach twisted into a tight, ugly knot. Not only was Kyle a faster racer, but Ryan noticed that he now had a *new* go-kart -- *a special Tony Kart from Italy* -- painted in bright red, with flames down the side pods outlined in gold, and a skull and crossbones on both sides of the nose piece. It was also mounted on a kart stand with a hydraulic lift, so no one had to lift it. Ryan's own kart was not brand-new, but it was a competitive one, bought from a former karting champion.

He *hated* Kyle's superior attitude! So did many of the other racers. But Kyle *was* tough to beat, and -- what was worse -- he knew it! Kyle gave Ryan another sneering look, then walked away.

"Don't let him get you down," said a firm voice behind Ryan. Turning, he saw it was Maria. She didn't race, but often came to watch her brother Arturo compete. She also helped Arturo work on his go-kart at home. Maria wanted to be an engineer someday.

"Kyle's a bully, and we all know it," she added. "Don't let him get under your skin."

Huh! Easier said than done, I'd love to punch him out! Ryan thought, as anger seeped into his brain. Every single driver on this track would like to beat Kyle for the year-end trophy, but at this point, it looked like a long-shot. This was the fifth race of the season, and Sampson had already earned the most points. He was well on his way to putting that cherished Waldron trophy on his *own* shelf, and *now he had a new kart!*

Carefully wheeling their kart stand, Ryan and his dad moved to the transponder area. For Timing and Scoring, the transponders would track each racer's elapsed time on-track during practice, qualifying, and the races. Expensive to buy, most kart racers rented them on race day. Ryan and his dad made sure their transponder was properly mounted. The rulebook stated that "it must be mounted on the inside of the left pod, nine to twelve inches from the rear of the centerline of the kingpin, to the leading edge of the transponder."

Next, at the tech area, Ryan waited nervously, shifting from foot to foot. No matter how hard a racer tried, sometimes there was just one little thing – a loose wire on the wheel, a number out of place, perhaps, that would keep them from passing inspection. Frank, the inspector, was going over the kart very carefully. Fuel was okay, wire clips properly installed on every wheel, tires properly inflated. Ryan's number "03" – he considered it lucky – accurately placed on his kart.

"Okay, son, everything's on the up-and-up; you're legal for today's racing," Frank said, flashing a friendly smile.

"Thanks!" Ryan said, grinning back. Frank waved his kart through. Once his kart cleared tech, Ryan always felt a huge sense of relief!

At the Driver's Meeting in Grid A, the race official reviewed all the safety rules. "If you're shown the blue flag with the diagonal stripe," he announced, "that means that a faster kart is overtaking you. If you can, point to the side on which you want them to safely pass you. Do *not* change your racing line. Then it's the responsibility of the overtaking driver to pass you safely." After answering a few questions from the racers, he finished the meeting. With happy yells, the racers rushed toward their pits. Time to go racing!

Ryan's first practice lap was great. His second two-lap stint was even better. Boy, he was eager to qualify! He'd show that Kyle Sampson a thing or two! Then, just before qualifying, he noticed something important. His kart's left front tire was a little soft. It needed more air. "Dad, will you get our SCUBA tank out of the truck? We need it to inflate this tire." There were other ways to inflate the tires, but some racers used those tanks; it was faster and easier.

A few minutes later, his dad was back, a puzzled look on his face. Their tank was missing! It was nowhere in the truck! Ryan's stomach churned into that angry tight knot again! He couldn't qualify well on a soft tire. What were they going to do?

"Are you sure we packed it this morning?"

"I'm positive. It's marked off on our checklist. This is really strange."

Things were suddenly looking pretty grim. Thoughts of despair ran through Ryan's mind. "*What will we do? How can I qualify my best now?*" The angry knot in his stomach grew even tighter. He got it whenever he felt threatened by Kyle's winning, and he *hated* it!

A voice suddenly brought him to his senses.

"I think Arturo has an extra tank," Maria called over to him. Nearby, she had heard their nervous conversation. Hurrying to her own truck, she climbed into the back and began searching quickly around their tools. Her search lasted only a minute or two, but to Ryan it seemed like *f-o-r-e-v-e-r*! Finally, she came out of the truck. "There's plenty of air in both our tanks," she said, running back to them. "Arturo won't mind if you use this one."

The knot in Ryan's stomach quickly unwound. Later, they'd have to find their own missing tank. Quickly, his dad filled the tire to its' proper pressure, and checked the others. Ryan was ready to go!

Qualifying was hot and heavy. Kyle, as usual, was fastest, with Randy Kennedy second, Arturo Martinez third, and Ryan running fourth through the first lap. Throttling through Turn 10, Ryan finally managed to slip past Arturo to take third. Then he neatly maneuvered through on the inside of the hairpin, passed Randy, and was running Kyle down when qualifying ended. He was now second on the grid for the Pre-Main.

Once again, Kyle sent a sneer his way. "You think you're fast, but I'll wipe you out in the Pre-Main," he warned.

Ryan knew he meant it. He had to reach down deep and pull up his own confidence, but boy, he'd sure like to get the best of Kyle!

"Don't let him fool you with his bluster," his dad said, back at the pits. "You ran a fine qualifying race. You can do even better, and beat him."

His dad was his rock. He built up Ryan's hopes whenever he got down. Again, they gave the kart a once-over. Everything was ready. At the signal from the race official, they wheeled their kart into Grid B. Soon, another official motioned them forward to Grid A, ready to start.

In Grid A, they lifted his kart off the stand, lowering it into his second-place line-up. His dad swiftly rolled the stand back to their pit. Ryan visualized himself in Victory Circle after today's race. "I most definitely can do it," he told himself." I'll show that stinkin' Kyle!"

Earlier at their pit, Ryan had put on all his equipment. Even that was done with a checklist. His dad called off each item; Ryan responded.

Fire-retardant socks? "Check."

High-top shoes? "Check."

Driving suit? "Check."

Protective neck brace? "Check."

Snell-approved safety helmet? "Check."

Gloves? "Check."

The weather had heated up since morning. Ryan knew that wearing all his equipment in the heat would be uncomfortable, but it was necessary for his own safety. He climbed into his kart. On his helmet was a cherished autograph – right next to the American flag! It was from famed Indianapolis 500 winner Rick Spears. Spears had won the Indianapolis 500 -- *four times*! Now retired from racing, he was coaching young, upcoming Indy 500 drivers.

CHAPTER FOUR

Ryan smiled as he remembered when he was just six. He and his dad were watching a television documentary about the Indianapolis 500 on the famed 2.5-mile oval track. That was the year that Rick Spears won that prestigious race -- for his *fourth* time! Ryan loved the intense speed of the cars, the ear-splitting sound, and the tremendous skill all the drivers had behind the wheel. That documentary had seared itself into his memory, and Spears became his instant hero. Even at that early age, Ryan felt then that he wanted to race in the Indianapolis 500 someday.

Years later, Ryan actually met Spears at the Indianapolis 500. That particular race was even more historic than ever. As a gift for his thirteenth birthday, his dad had taken him to Indy -- *for the 100th Running of the Indianapolis 500!* Spears did not usually sign autographs – he was too busy training drivers – but a friendly Indy 500 official had forwarded to Spears a special autograph request from Ryan's dad.

With a whole hour to wait for that meeting, Ryan and his dad hurried over to the Indianapolis Motor Speedway Hall of Fame Museum. They wanted to survey all the famous race cars – and also see the Borg-Warner Trophy. Ryan had seen photos of it on-line, but when he worked his way through the massive crowds and saw that actual majestic sterling silver trophy, he sucked in his breath! Wow! His eyes quickly scanned the sculpted faces of the famous winners, noting the year each one won the Indianapolis 500, and their average speed of that race.

A.J. Foyt was on there; so was Al Unser, Sr. They had also won the Indianapolis 500 *four times*! Ryan finally found the face of the driver he idolized the most, the third four-time winner -- Rick Spears! Ryan glued Spears' sculpted image into his mind. *Could he himself* be on that trophy someday – *especially four times*? Just then he felt a tap on his shoulder. The guard told them Spears was waiting for them over at the garage area.

That wait had been well worth it. Spears met them with a warm and friendly smile.

"What kind of racer are you, son?" he asked.

"I'm a kart racer right now," Ryan said, "but I want to race in the Indianapolis 500 someday – and win, just like you."

"That's great," Spears replied, with a grin. He liked Ryan's spirit. "If you continue to work at it, get plenty of seat time in race cars, and focus on doing your extreme best, I'm sure you'll succeed." After a few more words of advice, he took Ryan's helmet, and quickly autographed it. Handing it back to him, he said, with a friendly wink, "This is just for you. Hope to see you in the Indy 500 someday."

Thrilled to have his hero's autograph, Ryan quickly glanced at the words. They read, "To a future winner – Ryan," followed by that prized signature, "Rick Spears."

"You bet! I'll definitely follow your instructions, Rick," Ryan blurted out, "and thanks a million for your autograph!"

Next, he and his dad eagerly joined the massive crowd on the famed Indianapolis oval racetrack, before the race. With 350,000 race fans attending that special anniversary event, it was new, exciting, incredible... Electric starters were being tested on the race cars; the whine of lug-nut guns also shrilled through the air... The Purdue Band was there in full regalia, ready to play, the Color Guard was ready to present America's flag, a disc jockey was happily spinning records, the cluster of colorful balloons was ready to go up, the drivers were eagerly waiting off-track for their time to race...

Ryan and his dad soaked up every single wonderful, dazzling sight and sound. As the Indy cars were pushed into place on the grid, they intently studied every detail of those powerful machines – the aerodynamic shape of the car bodies, the angles of the front and rear wings set to provide downforce, the shape and size of the tires.

Ryan was truly amazed at all the intricate equipment he saw, especially the imposing large cluster of electronic buttons on the Indy cars' steering wheels.

"Look, Dad! Those steering wheels are definitely high-tech computers in the cockpits."

Working their way through the immense throngs of race fans, they headed toward one special destination – the prized row of bricks at the start-finish line. When they finally made it, Ryan's dad turned to him.

"Okay, champ! Here's your chance! Get down and kiss those bricks like these drivers do when they win! You can practice today for when you win here someday!" Kneeling down, they both kissed the historic row of bricks -- a memory they would cherish forever, and a promising start to Ryan's open-wheel future.

The track guards blew their whistles; it was time to clear the grid. One hour 'til the start!

As if by magic, the massive crowd morphed rapidly from the grid into the stands. Each driver was announced, then was carefully strapped into their car. As the rookies' names were announced to the eager crowd –*Alexander Rossi, Max Chilton, Matt Brabham, Spencer Pigot, Stephan Wilson* – Ryan visualized himself being introduced as an Indy 500 rookie, someday.

When the patriotic words and melody of the United States' National Anthem had filled the air, salty tears formed in Ryan's eyes. He was so proud to be here! So proud of his country! So proud of his dad!

Then – those famous words to start the race rang out to the crowd:

Dri-vers! Start – your -- en-gines!

A huge roar went up from the crowd! 33 powerful V-6 engines roared to life! Ryan's heart took a huge leap!

The green flag waved, and those 33 cars shot into speedy action! Ryan Hunter-Reay charged from third to first, grabbing the lead from pole-sitter James Hinchcliffe! Ryan intently watched the 33 drivers battle intensely through every lap -- some gaining positions by passing at just the right time -- but he soon began to notice rookie Alexander Rossi. Rossi had seven years of Formula One and road-course experience, but just a couple months' training in oval-track racing. Yet, in his *first* Indy 500, Rossi had managed to qualify 11th, and was now definitely holding his own. Two slow pit stops – fueling problems with a stuck fuel probe – dropped him way back during the race, once to 29th.

Still, Rossi had managed to battle his way *to the lead – twice*! In the final few laps, Josef Newgarden and Carlos Munoz kept swapping the lead, but near the very end they both had to pit for fuel, and Rossi – for the third time -- swept into the lead! Good pit-stop timing during the race by his car's co-owner Bryan Herta -- *plus Rossi's driving talent and the grueling, but clever, saving of fuel that he did in those final laps –* brought him home the victor!

He beat teammate Carlos Munoz by 4.4975 seconds, ran out of fuel after he crossed the finish line, then needed a splash of fuel to get his race car to Victory Circle for his celebration! Along with the crowd, Ryan and his dad were up on their feet when Rossi won, yelling with excitement, thrusting their fists in the air! *A rookie – had just won the 100th Running of the Indianapolis 500!* This race was truly *The Greatest Spectacle in Racing*!

During their long drive back home, Ryan was extremely quiet, intently replaying the race over and over in his mind to study new racing skills. He had also *seen a rookie win the 500*, had *seen the majestic Borg-Warner Trophy in person*, and best of all – *received a terrific autograph from his racing hero, Rick Spears!* What an outstanding thirteenth-birthday gift this had been! Looking over at his dad, he expressed his sincere thanks.

"This trip has certainly taught me a lot, Dad," he added. "I realize I have a *ton* of learning and racing to do if I plan to race at Indy someday." His father responded with a grin.

We'll keep working hard on that, he thought to himself.

CHAPTER FIVE

Now every time Ryan was back at Atlas to compete, he would smile at Spears' words. He'd reach up and pat that treasured autograph, then start his engine. *Now, he was always ready for combat!* And the green flag waved for another race to begin!

At the green, Kyle Sampson grabbed the lead, with Ryan close on his rear. Through Turn 1, Turn 2 – Ryan held tight onto second. Then Kyle began pulling away, his powerful new go-kart stretching out the distance between them. Turn 5, Turn 6 -- through the Benson Bend Curve – Kyle was pulling away even more.

Flooring the pedal, Ryan took all the right lines through the curves, over the rumble strips, full throttle.

Kyle was still pulling away. After a few more laps, Ryan began closing, making up more time through the turns, closing the gap. On Lap 6, he finally caught up with Kyle – and roared past him! He was in the lead!

Kyle was having none of that! Fighting to regain first place, he pulled up on the rear of Ryan's kart, trying to force him to make a mistake. Ryan held on, gripped his steering wheel tighter, pulled away again. Kyle closed in again. It was a dogfight between the two. Other racers and their families were shouting from the bleachers.

"Go, Ryan, you can beat Kyle! We know you can!" Those were sweet sounds to Ryan, but they angered Kyle. Suddenly, slightly out of the sight of the Race Director due to the high tents and trailers, Kyle made a swift move. He drove up close to Ryan's kart, trying again to take the air off the rear. Gripping his wheel tighter, Ryan drove away. In the same place on the next lap, Kyle drove as close as he dared without touching Ryan's kart. Suddenly, Ryan felt his kart losing its' grip! He felt it skidding – spinning out of control! He tried his best to save it, finally did, but Kyle charged past him, and took the checkered flag!

Ryan was so angry he could spit nails! He had just lost precious points! He'd make Kyle pay for that! Back in his pit, he climbed out of his kart, yanked off his helmet and gloves, and headed off towards Kyle.

"Hey, where you going?" yelled his dad.

"To settle a score with Kyle! That's where!" he shouted, as he marched toward his hated competitor. Kyle saw Ryan coming -- with fire in his eyes! He turned and ran – behind the officials' building. But Ryan was too quick. Catching up to Kyle, he grabbed him, spun him around, pulled back his arm, and was ready to give Kyle a solid punch on his jaw!

Startled, Kyle covered his face.

Suddenly, Ryan came to his senses! He knew if he got in a fight and hit Kyle, he'd be barred from the racing series forever! Instead, his instincts took over. "You dirty dog!" he yelled at Kyle, giving him a hefty shove. "You spun me out on purpose! You're nothin' but a creep!"

"I did nothing of the sort! You're just a lousy racer! You spun yourself out, and now you're trying to blame it on me!"

By that time, other racers had come behind the building, clustered in a bunch, hoping to see a fight. "Go get him, Ryan! He's had this coming! Shove him again!"

Ryan's arm shot forward to give Kyle another hard shove.

Suddenly, a strong pair of arms grabbed both of his, and dragged him backwards! It was Ryan's dad.

"What are you *thinking?* You know you shouldn't fight!' his father yelled. "You know you shouldn't resort to violence!"

"I know!" Ryan yelled back, as he tried to calm himself down. "It's just that I'm so stinkin' tired of his taunting, and now his cheating. He took me out on purpose!"

"That still doesn't mean that you should pick a fight!" His father's face was red with frustration. Ryan was puzzled; he had never seen his dad angry like this. After all, it was just a simple shove. What's more, he felt he got the best of Kyle.

Ryan and Kyle soon found themselves inside the officials' building. It was Kyle's word against Ryan's. "I don't know how he spun out," Kyle said, with a false innocent look. "All of a sudden, he was gone, so I took the lead."

Ryan was *smoldering* inside! Kyle was lying, and since no official had seen his action due to the high tents blocking their vision in that area of the track, Ryan had no proof. Corner workers were called in, but no one had seen the actual incident. Kyle was still off the hook!

They both got a stern warning. One more action like this would take all their points away, and they'd be suspended forever from racing in that series! Then they were both given a one-race suspension for acting up at the track, and sent back to their pits. That suspension would start on the next weekend of racing.

Ryan was still fuming. "I don't know how, but I'll get him taken care of," he told himself. "I'll definitely find a way!" In the Main race that day, Kyle won again, of course. Ryan promised himself even more revenge.

When he got home, Ryan got another strong scolding – from his mother! His dad had told her the whole story.

"Ryan, you've been taught better than that!" she yelled. At those harsh words, he felt really bad inside. He'd never seen his parents so angry before. Now that he was home, he realized how foolish he'd been. "I'm sorry," he said. "I guess I just lost my temper."

"I guess you certainly did," said his mom. "Now let's have some dinner, and decide how to proceed from here."

He certainly *had* to plan how to proceed. His reckless action had now put him under suspension. He was not allowed to race – *for one whole week*! That would certainly lose him more points toward the championship!

In his bedroom, Ryan had lots of time to think about the foolish thing he'd done. He'd never been under suspension before. He couldn't race, so there was no need to work on his kart, once he'd get it cleaned up. As he looked over it later in the garage, it had no damage – just lots of dirt all over. He was lucky. Sadly, he began the clean-up.

One whole week's suspension! What was he going to do? How could he earn points if he couldn't race?

Then he got a silly grin on his face. There *was* one bright side to this! Kyle couldn't race, so *he* couldn't earn points, either. It was a predicament for them both!

Just then, his dad came into the garage. "Son, I've been thinking. One, I'm sorry that I got so angry at you at the track. And Two, I know you're worrying about not earning any points for this week, with only a few races left in the season."

Listening to those words, Ryan really felt the brunt of his foolishness. As angry as he'd been at Kyle, he should never have picked that fight! Now he had only penalized what he worked so hard to gain! He was completely disgusted with himself!

His dad spoke again. "There *is* a way we can work this out. Let's get out the rulebook." Ryan wondered where this was headed. "You can earn points as a worker."

Ryan had never thought of that. He had always been at the track to race, not to work.

Opening the rulebook, his dad began to read: JUNIOR DRIVERS – Must be present at the event and have an adult work alongside him or her during their work assignment, issued by the Race Director. Working Drivers must sign in at the Entry Booth for the class, or classes, they are working for. A driver will be credited for the class they are working for at the end of the day they work.

Any member who shows up to a South-Cal race with the Intent To Race, has paid their entry fee, but

<u>HAS NOT PUT THEIR KART OR THEMSELVES</u>
<u>IN A KART, ON THE TRACK, MAY WORK</u>.

That was it! He could still earn points, even if he couldn't race! That would keep him in the game!

That Saturday, Ryan woke up early. A tap sounded on his door. Sparkplug sat up to see who was there. Ryan did, too.

His dad poked his head inside. "Time to rise and shine! Have to get to the track early, before all the jobs are gone."

His clock said 6 a.m. They wanted to be there no later than 7. Ryan remembered that the work line formed really early. Rushing into the bathroom, he washed up as fast as he could.

They each had breakfast and grabbed their lunch, which Mom packed the night before, and dashed out the door. On the way, Ryan wondered what kind of work assignment he'd get.

During that week, he had mowed lawns again to earn his entry fee. Today, he had to pay that fee although he wasn't allowed to race. *That's okay,* he thought to himself. *I can still earn those much-needed points.*

At 7 a.m., the track was already humming with activity. Luckily, they were early enough. Not many racers were registered to work. Ryan was fifth in line. At his turn, he stepped up to the window.

"Good morning. I'm here to pay, and work for the day," he told the registration clerk. Next, he was sent to the Racing Director. "What kind of job do you have for me?"

"Looks like I have a perfect assignment for you," said the director. "You can help weigh the karts when they come off the track to make sure they're legal weight."

After practice, qualifying, and each race, every kart was brought to the scale. Each driver pushed his kart onto the scale, then stepped on the scale with both feet. If they were under the legal weight limit, that kart would be disqualified for certain races. One after another, Ryan helped pass karts onto the scale, under the guidance of the official. So far, all of them had passed. Then Zane Ritchey pushed his kart forward...

Zane was another racer Ryan did not like. For some unknown reason, he'd often block Ryan on the track when Ryan was trying to make a pass. Basically, he seemed like a good kid, but there was just something odd about him. Ryan couldn't quite figure out what it was. On the scale, Zane and his kart were legal.

Ryan was tempted to sneak his foot under the scale, just enough to lift it and put that kart under legal weight. It was so-o-o tempting, but at the last moment, he didn't. That really wouldn't be fair. Still, he had his doubts about Zane. He and Kyle were driven to the track together to race, so he might be in cahoots with Kyle. It was just a sneaking suspicion, something he felt deep down inside. The official leveled the scale; Zane pushed his kart off. The next racer moved forward.

That work kept Ryan busy all day. When it was time to finish, the official gave him a hearty pat on the back. "Great job, Ryan! You can help me again anytime you want!" he said with a grin.

"Oh, no!" Ryan shot back. "I don't plan to be in a position where I'm not allowed to race -- ever again."

On the way home, Ryan told his dad how close he came to cheating to put Zane and his kart in jeopardy, but he didn't.

His father never said a word. Secretly, he was proud of his son. He had done the right thing on his own.

As they drove, Ryan was tallying his new points in his head...

Pulling into the driveway, they saw Ryan's mom in the yard, a distressed look on her face. She loved to garden, and was known to have the prettiest rose bushes in the entire neighborhood. She should, with the hours of feeding, pruning, and loving care she gave them.

Ryan jumped out of the truck. His mom was usually a cheerful and happy person, so he was puzzled.

"What's wrong?"

She wiped her forehead with her gardening glove. "I'm not sure, but something's happening to my Pink Lady rose bush."

"Like what?"

"The leaves look a little brown, and the buds aren't opening like they normally do."

"Your other roses?"

"They're blooming just fine. It's just the Pink Lady." That was her favorite, a possible prize winner this year. She was so proud of her rose garden next to the garage. She'd fill the house with the blooms until it smelled like a garden inside. She enjoyed three things -- cooking, her roses, and her charities.

"I hate to say this," she said, "but it looks like there's been some digging around that bush. I'm inclined to think that it's your dog, Sparkplug. Westies do like to dig, you know."

Ryan's heart sank. He never thought his *pet* would cause any trouble.

"Come over here and see," she said. He and his dad knelt down. Sure enough, the ground was dug up, right near the roots of the bush, and the bush looked like it was struggling.

"Maybe if you give it some more plant food?" Ryan suggested.

"I did that last week, but it's just not responding."

Ryan felt the sad tone in her voice. She'd been grooming the Pink Lady for the River Valley Rose Show that next weekend. Thinking hard, he came up with the best idea he could. "Here's what we'll do, Mom. Dad and I will put a little wire fence around that bush. Then Sparkplug won't be able to dig around it."

Her face brightened a little. "That might work," she said. "Let's give that a try."

He and his dad made a quick trip to the hardware store. Soon the small fence was in place, deep in the soil around the entire rose bush. "That ought to do it," his dad said, brushing dirt off his hands.

"Well, thank you both. I sure would hate to lose my favorite."

Ryan made a mental note: *When Sparkplug's out in the yard with me, be sure to keep him away from Mom's roses.*

The next Saturday he got up early, and headed into the garage.

"Ryan! Come back here!" called his mom from the kitchen. "No go-kart work today! You have to help me at the Rose Show like you did last year!"

"The Rose Show? But your Pink Lady is all brown and not doing well!"

"I know. So I've decided to enter my Rosaflora instead. It's in perfect bloom."

Ryan slammed his fist against the garage wall. "But, Mom, you know how I *hate* to go there and serve lemonade. I'm always afraid I'll spill it on someone!"

"Don't screw up your face like that, Ryan! I volunteered you a month ago, as usual. Now go put on your nice white shirt and dark trousers. And be sure your hair is neatly combed."

"Dang it about wearing trousers! Why can't I just wear my jeans?"

"Because this is a formal occasion, and you know from last year that jeans just won't do."

With disgust in his heart, he ran up to his room to change.

One hour later, they were on their way, with his mother's nicest Rosaflora blossoms in the car. His stiff starchy shirt rubbed annoyingly against his neck. He'd be glad when this day was over.

Inside the huge tent, he was assigned to six tables, serving their lemonade. At the front of the tent were two tables -- one for the entries, and one full of trophies. Ryan was sent into the private screened serving area, emerging soon with a tray full of pitchers of iced lemonade. He served the women at the first table. When they smiled and thanked him, he blushed red in the face. Ugh! He wanted to be anywhere but here! But, for his mom's sake, he'd try to make the best of it.

Coming out of the serving area with his second tray, Ryan suddenly stopped in his tracks! Coming the other way was Kyle Sampson, carrying a tray of empty lemonade pitchers in his hands! What the heck was *he* doing here?

Spotting a large potted palm, Ryan squeezed way behind it before Kyle passed. If Kyle ever saw him, he'd tease him forever! Besides, what the heck was Kyle even doing at this Rose Show? Carefully, all morning, Ryan would serve, then hide behind the palm, a decorative pillar -- anything handy, so he couldn't be spotted by Sampson.

Then it happened! A woman let out a loud shriek! Crouched behind a pillar, Ryan saw that Kyle had accidentally spilled some lemonade on the lady's dress! To keep from laughing out loud, Ryan clamped his hand down hard over his mouth. Now *he* really had some embarrassing words to throw at Kyle if he gave him a hard time at the track! "Hey, fellow racers, here comes Kyle Sampson, the clumsy kid who spilled lemonade on a lady's dress!" *That* would fix him, if he gave Ryan trouble!

When the luncheon and judging were over, Ryan breathed a sigh of relief. He and his mom headed home, her trophy for her Rosaflora blooms proudly perched on the seat between them.

She was happy and smiling. Her entry had won Second Place. She could hardly wait to tell Dad. Although he'd really hated going to the rose show, Ryan smiled, too. It was nice to see Mom so happy about her prize. That was her form of competition, and she deserved a trophy for all her hard work, too. But he hoped she'd never volunteer him again. "I'm a racer, not a waiter," he kept telling himself. And he never did tell her about the lemonade he poured around the potted palm instead of serving it so he could hurry up and finish.

CHAPTER SIX

The next race week was a special one. Word had gone around that Joe Yoshida was finally coming to race with them. Yoshida, the toughest on the northwest tracks! That meant everyone would have to race better than they ever did.

Ryan was happy about that – but, in a way -- he was also concerned. This was another new challenge for him, and he hoped he was up to it! If Yoshida was as tough as other racers had said, Ryan would not only be challenged by Kyle, but by Yoshida, too.

"I hear he's going to be a handful," he said to his dad, on their way to Atlas.

His father glanced over. "Not scaring you off, is he?"

"Nah, I'll just have to race better than ever," Ryan answered. He gave his dad a friendly nudge.

In the rear seat of the truck cab, Timmy piped up. "I bet you kin beat anybody you want to."

Ryan smiled. He could certainly use Timmy as his cheerleader.

"Your kart's a good one, I know, 'cuz I watch you work on it all the time, both of you."

Ryan smiled again. Timmy had become a good little friend. As a special treat, this was his first trip to the racetrack. Hanging around Timmy's neck was his new prized possession. The day before, there had been an excited knock on the Edwards' kitchen door.

It was Timmy, bursting with his news. "I came right over to show you!" he shouted, when they opened the door. "Looky what I got for my birthday from my grampa. It's a new dig'tal camera! I kin take all the pik-churs I want and my dad will teach me how to put 'em in his computer. He says I kin load 'em in."

Ryan chuckled at Timmy's enthusiasm. "You mean you can upload them, Timmy."

"Yeah, whatever. And I have a two-giga... giga..."

"Gigabyte card to take your pictures on," Ryan chimed in.

"Yeah, whatever that is. I kin take a bunch of pik-churs on that tiny little card. I think that's pretty special. I wanna be a de-tek-tiv some day, and this'll get me started. I kin take pik-churs of the crim-nuls." His eyes sparkled again behind his glasses.

Somehow, Ryan felt that Timmy would definitely make a great detective. He had a curious and clever mind, and loved scientific things. He also emphasized all the words he felt were important.

As they neared the track, Ryan's mind went back to Joe Yoshida. Just how good would he be here on a new road-course where he had never raced? He'd soon find out.

They parked, got their entry card for their assigned pit location, and began unloading Ryan's kart.

Timmy was already out of the truck, clicking pictures of Ryan and his dad setting up their pit, unloading the kart, recording everything he could with his new "dig'tal."

Ryan was eager to get back behind the wheel. He had done that weigh-scale work to gain those points he'd lost while serving his penalty. Thinking back, he had to chuckle about that day.

That weekend, Kyle had also worked for points. He'd been given a different job, one he apparently hated -- a runner for the Results Board. That was where the officials posted the racers' times after every practice, qualifying, and race. Kyle had to go to the scorer's stand, pick up the latest time results, then run over and pin them up on the Results Board.

Due to the high temperatures that day, that turned out to be a hot and sweaty job, and every time that Ryan glanced over, Kyle had been shooting him dirty looks, as if he'd rather have been working at the weigh scale.

Ryan had felt a little smug inside. *It was good for Kyle to sweat a little,* he thought. *He'd always had it too easy and too good, anyway. He was the one whose folks had all the money...*

Although he'd never seen Kyle's folks, Kyle never seemed to lack for anything. He and his friend Zane always arrived at the track in the newest and best truck there. They were always driven to the track by the same man who then sat in the bleachers, stop-watching them as they raced. Between events, he'd work on their karts while they watched. Kyle always had the newest and best equipment. His kart with the hydraulic lift, his racing uniform, were always the most expensive a person could buy.

Zane didn't have all the finest stuff that Kyle had, but he also had very expensive equipment. He and Kyle even looked a little alike – red hair, a ruddy face, medium build. And worst of all, they were very close buddies. They always hung around together at the track, and at the food bar, enjoying mustard-slathered hot dogs, chips, and an icy cool drink, between races.

Ryan thought about the dozens of chores he'd done, just to be able to race. From what he was told,

Kyle, on the other hand, never had to do a thing – just go to school -- a private one, at that! *Some people get all the breaks in life*, he thought to himself.

"Look at this neat pik-chur I got!" Timmy broke Ryan's train of thought. "It's a pik-chur of Kyle Sampson's kart!" Ryan saw that Timmy could also be a pest. He glanced quickly at the image Timmy was showing him in his camera. "Yeah, yeah, it's a good picture. Now be careful not to get in anyone's way! Stay around our pit and out of trouble, okay?"

Missing the annoyance in Ryan's voice, Timmy agreed. "Sure, Ryan. Gee, this place is excitin.' I'm gonna see what else I kin shoot with my new camera!" He headed off again.

"Don't go too far away, stay right around here," Ryan reminded him, "and be careful of the trucks pulling into the track."

"Yeah, I will. I promise." But he was off again, clicking away, Ryan noticed, at just about everything that moved.

Suddenly, there was a hush around the track. Joe Yoshida was arriving. Everyone paused in their pits. Yoshida's truck was very large. Lettered on the side were the words – in gold: "Joe Yoshida. Northwest Karting Champion." He certainly came in style.

Ryan strained to get a look at this tough new competitor. But he couldn't see anything. *Strange*, he thought. *The truck's windows are tinted. I can't see who's inside.* Then he shrugged it off. "Must be just a preference," he said to himself. Maybe just another way a driver acts when he's a champion. He made a mental note to himself: *When I'm champion, I'll be riding into a track with my head out the window, waving and smiling.*

Then he realized – Yoshida was a Japanese name, and the Japanese were usually conservative. That must be the reason for the tinted windows. A modest way to behave, even if you are a champion.

After Yoshida's truck passed, Ryan and his dad got to work. He had not one -- but two -- racers he had to beat this weekend.

With Yoshida's arrival, the buzz had gone all around the track. A pit was assigned for this new racer.

"Yahoo," whooped Ryan. "Yoshida's entry pass is pitting him right next to Kyle!" He saw the look on Kyle's face when the new truck pulled into place. "I wonder just what Kyle's thinking?" At that moment, he'd loved to be able to look inside Kyle's brain. Was he threatened by this new arrival? Or, like Ryan, was he more determined to race harder than ever to beat this new guy?

They'd soon find out. An Asian man climbed out of the driver's side of the truck. *Must be Joe's father,* Ryan thought, as the man unloaded Yoshida's kart. Aha! It too was on a hydraulic lift -- Kyle had some competition there already! He watched Kyle frown. Deep down inside, Ryan forgot the threat of this new racer. He was enjoying Kyle's unhappy expression.

Looks like this guy has even more money than Kyle, he thought. He watched closely to see Kyle's next reaction when Yoshida'd come out of his truck. But that reaction never came. For some reason, Yoshida never came out...

The man set up Yoshida's pit, worked on his kart, and prepped everything to get ready for first practice. He also took the kart through pre-tech. Yoshida had still not come out of his truck...

Boy, thought Ryan, *I guess everyone does your work for you when you're a champion.* Then he looked over at his dad. "I'll never behave like that when I win the title." And then, he reminded himself, he'd better race well this weekend if he was going to become a champion!

Just then, an angry official, with Timmy in tow, rushed over to Ryan's pit.

"Is this your little brother?" he asked, in a loud voice.

"No, he's my next-door neighbor," Ryan said. "Why?"

"Well, whoever he is, if you brought him here, you better be responsible for him," said the official, in an angry tone.

"What seems to be the trouble?" Ryan asked, as his dad looked on in surprise.

"He's all over the place, taking pictures with his dang camera; that's what's the trouble! I just yanked him out of Grid B, where he was taking pictures of the go-karts, and getting in everyone's way. You know no one's supposed to be in Grid B except racers and officials!"

The official was right. So how could Ryan concentrate on his racing and keep track of Timmy, too? It had been a big mistake to bring him to the track.

Just then, Maria came rushing over. "I'll look after him while you race," she said. "I have a brother at home about his age, and know how to keep him under control. I can do the same with Timmy."

Ryan shot Maria a look of gratitude. His dad also looked relieved.

As she led Timmy away, they heard her say, "C'mon. I'll take you up on the hill, where you can get some great pictures of Ryan on the racetrack. It'll be good for you to learn how to use that neat camera to photograph go-karts racing at high speed."

Whew! Maria to the rescue again, Ryan thought...

Everyone was still waiting for Joe Yoshida to appear. It was almost time for first practice. Finally, the door opened on the champion's truck. Yoshida stepped out, completely dressed in his safety gear.

Ryan quickly noticed something different from all the other racers. Yoshida wore a balaclava -- a protective woven cloth head sock -- under his helmet. Only his eyes were showing. Even Kyle didn't wear a balaclava. But it was in the rules that one could be worn.

Ryan noticed something else about Yoshida. He was smaller than the other racers.

Hmmm, he thought. *I know lots of Asians are small, so I guess I shouldn't be surprised.* "Although he's smaller," Ryan reminded himself, "he's already a champion, so he's probably powerful on the racetrack. We'll see what he can do in this first practice."

That one was a real eye-opener. Missing the last race, Ryan had practiced twice that week. During those sessions, he had clocked times two-tenths of a second faster than he'd ever done before. Today, the track was "green," with no tire rubber laid down on it. Rain had washed it off the day before, so Ryan and his dad had put on new tires – new slicks -- for better grip.

With his kart now through tech, Ryan finally moved up to Grid A. It was just his luck; Yoshida was on the grid right next to him. At first this worried Ryan, but then he realized that it was the perfect chance to see just what this guy could do. And who was third on the grid? Kyle Sampson, of course, with Zane Ritchey fourth. All competitive drivers, set to show what their best would be.

At the official's signal, Ryan gunned his engine, and moved onto the track. Soon all twenty drivers were out on the course, eager to practice. Ryan began running faster around the course. Suddenly, the kart driven by Yoshida charged alongside him, then shot ahead. "Wow!" Ryan said. "That guy can really move!" Soon all four – Yoshida, Ryan, Kyle, and Zane – were zipping around the course, sometimes side-by-side, sometimes nose-to-tail. But it was mostly Yoshida who led them all!

Coming up beside him heading into the turn, Ryan gunned his engine, indicated that he was ready to make a pass, but Yoshida closed the door on him, and kept the lead. "Holy, moley! This is only practice, but this guy drives like he's racing for the trophy!" Ryan muttered inside his helmet.

Kyle was closing fast. Ryan wanted to make a move, but Ernie Farlow, motoring around at his own slower pace, was in the way. Finally, Ryan was able to pass him, but now it was Zane who was running side-by-side, and Kyle had fallen slightly back. Yoshida? He was still up front, until the checkered flag waved to end the session.

By now one thing was perfectly clear to Ryan and all the other contenders. Yoshida was going to be hard to beat! In the second practice, Ryan took the lead, but lost it again to Yoshida before that session ended.

Boy, he thought, *this guy's so good that we all have our work cut out for us! Even though he's not racing for the championship, he's certainly eager to win – every single time!*

During that second practice, Ryan formed his own plan. Since Yoshida was so fast, Ryan followed him again for as many laps as possible, studying every line he took around the track. He even learned a new thing or two about how to navigate the hairpin turn, carving out an extra tenth of a second there.

Qualifying was even tougher. Yoshida had stepped up his performance even more, and Ryan was struggling now to keep up with him. Joe knew every trick of the trade – he was good – and Ryan found that *he* still had lessons to learn.

No one expected Yoshida to take the pole in qualifying. He had never driven there before; didn't know all the twists and turns of this course. But somehow he did! Now Ryan really had to buckle down, and drive smarter than ever! At least, he'd qualified second. Zane, to everyone's surprise, was third, Kyle fourth.

What happened to Kyle? Had he lost his confidence with this new competitor on the course? Not really. Turned out he was having a problem with the chain on his kart. Back in his pit, his attendant worked on it as Kyle watched. He got it back through tech in time for the Pre-Main.

CHAPTER SEVEN

Where the racers finished in the Pre-Main set their starting position in the Main. *It would look really bad if Yoshida won that pole,* Ryan thought. The other racers were probably thinking the same thing. It looked like the qualifying session was shaping up to be a free-for-all. There would probably be some close racing, even some banging around, but everyone would have to be careful that they didn't cross the line into illegal driving. If they did, it would mean disqualification for that weekend.

At the green, Kyle Sampson, his kart now working just fine, charged into the lead. Ryan was fast on his tail. Yoshida was third, Zane fourth, with the rest of the field spread out behind in the grid. There were only eight laps to capture that pole, and Kyle was already moving away from the pack.

Ryan was running hard, taking as tight a line as he could around the circuit. Catching up to Kyle, he raced beside him, but Kyle shot back into the lead.

Now Yoshida was closing in on both Ryan and Kyle, his kart charging around the asphalt course like he had run there forever.

Man, that guy's a quick study! Ryan thought. He was right. Yoshida was taking the shortest line through every single curve, moving fast down the straight-away, and pulling ever closer to Ryan's bumper.

Kyle was still in the lead. Pushing his kart to the limit, Ryan fought to hold second, closing in inch-by-inch on Kyle. Suddenly, with a burst of speed, Yoshida was beside him. Determined not to let him pass, Ryan moved ahead again, eager to catch Kyle. Ryan really wanted that pole!

For seven laps they battled back and forth, Ryan finally leading, Yoshida passing them both, Kyle taking it back. The race fans and families at the track were all watching the hard-fought competition. Now this was real karting!

Finally, on Lap 8, Kyle found a new burst of speed, pulled away from the other two, and captured the pole!

"*Rats!*" Ryan said to himself. Still, he had finished second, and had held his own with Yoshida during those hard-fought eight laps. That proved he had what it takes to be a strong competitor. He had still stayed ahead of a champ.

Before the final, the top five finishers drew their tech numbers from a can. Ryan got No. 3; his kart passed tech with flying colors, he was ready to out-run the entire grid!

In that final, Kyle seemed rocket-powered, holding the lead at the green flag, charging far ahead of the rest of the field. Ryan's 125cc engine was running at full power, but he couldn't catch him. Yoshida, on Ryan's bumper again, seemed to be struggling this time to pass Ryan and overtake Kyle. Zane was now far back in the field, definitely not in this fight.

Kyle drove smoothly through the slower corner, holding a steady line, moving further ahead. Ryan, fighting for every second he could save, slipped carefully through the hairpin. He began closing in on Kyle. But Yoshida was not giving up. He fought just as hard, broad-sailing through every curved section of the track, giving Ryan all the trouble he could handle.

But Ryan had his eye on that win! It would be a big gain in points. On Lap 13 -- one away from the checkered -- he finally began to close the gap on Kyle. Soon they were running side-by-side, Ryan waiting for the end to make his final move. Then Kyle took the lead, but Ryan caught Kyle in the hair-pin, stuck his nose into second, slipped by him on the inside, and took the checkered flag! Kyle second,

Yoshida third. There was no knot in Ryan's stomach this time!

"Great job there, son," said his dad, with pride in his voice. "You certainly held your own in that one!" They headed for the weigh scale, pleased at how Ryan had come back after his suspension. Actually, that layoff had made him more determined than ever to do well.

At the track, the sun was getting low in the sky. His dad said, "We better find Maria and round up Timmy. I'm sure he got his share of racing pictures today."

Just as he said that, he heard Timmy yell, and saw him running down the hill, Maria not far behind. Timmy was waving something shiny over his head. "Wonder what mysterious object our de-tek-tiv has found now?" joked Ryan's dad. As he got closer, they were both surprised to see that it was a SCUBA tank.

Out of breath as he reached the bottom of the hill, Timmy huffed out, "I think it's yours, Ryan. It has your name on it!"

Sure enough! At the top of the tank was a label. It read: Property of Ryan Edwards, Edwards Racing Team. It was the tank that had disappeared from their truck a few weeks earlier! "Where did you find this, Timmy?" Ryan asked.

"Like I toldja, I'm a de-tek-tiv, and I like to look for clues and unusual things that kin solve a crime. I went to the top of the hill to take pik-churs of you all racing in that final. Then I got a stick and was pushin' things around up there, just lookin' for unusual stuff. This was lyin' in the deep weeds. If I hadn't pushed the weeds aside, I'da never found it."

Ryan and his Dad frowned. How had their tank disappeared from their truck and been found up at the top of the hill? "Maria, do you have any idea what happened here?" asked Ryan's dad.

"No, I sure don't,' she replied. "I was watching the racing and after Timmy took all the pictures he wanted, he began exploring around up there. That's when he found it."

"You do make a good detective," Ryan told Timmy. "Now it's up to you to find out how it got from our truck to the top of that hill."

"You bet I will," Timmy said, pleased about his find. "I'll uncover every clue 'til I kin tell you 'zactly what happened."

Ryan and his Dad were pleased to have their SCUBA tank back, and Timmy was truly serious about solving this mystery. But could he track the culprit down?

On their way home, Timmy was in deep thought. "Y'know, if I'm a good kid and work hard, my parents might buy me a fingerprint kit," he said. "Then I kin tell you who the person was that took your SCUBA tank."

In the front seat, Ryan quietly laughed to himself. This kid's really serious, he thought. If Timmy had such a kit, he'd probably solve it for sure. Ryan wanted it solved, too. He could not figure out who could have taken that tank from their truck – or how? Timmy didn't know that all their truck doors – front and back -- were always locked when they were out on the track. No one could have broken in without their knowing. They had a true mystery on their hands...

CHAPTER EIGHT

. . . Ryan was on the podium. He raised his treasured trophy in one hand far above his head, punching it toward the sky as high as he could reach. His mom and dad were in the front of the crowd, laughing and smiling, cheering that he had finally won the season title. Timmy was taking all kinds of photos of him with his dig'tal camera...

Bang! Bang! Bang! There was loud pounding on his bedroom door. Startled, Ryan sat up. *Where was he???* He rubbed his eyes. *Where was the trophy???* Looking around, he realized he was in his bedroom! But what about the title? What about the trophy? Suddenly he realized that it had all been...a dream.

Bang! Bang! Bang! There was loud pounding on his door again. A voice came booming through the door.

"You going to sleep all day? The sun's up already!"

It was Uncle John! *What's he doing here?* Ryan thought. He leaped out of bed. As he opened the door, Uncle John's fist was ready to bang on the door again, his arm stopped in mid-air.

"What's goin' on?" Ryan asked.

"What's going on?" repeated Uncle John. "It's a beautiful day, the sun is up, and you and I, my boy, are going fishing! You have no racing today, your mom said you don't have any chores to do around the house or the neighborhood, so you – and I – are going fishing!"

Ryan hated to lose that wonderful championship dream. But as he cleared his mind, he grinned. There was nothing he enjoyed -- other than racing -- than fishing with his dad and Uncle John.

"Hurry and wash up!" Uncle John said. "And be sure to wear your khaki clothes. You don't want to scare any of the fish with that bright red flannel shirt of yours!"

Ryan knew what that meant. Bright colors scared the trout away, and if they decided to cast while standing in the stream, they would catch no fish that day. Rummaging in his closet, he grabbed his khaki shirt and pants, and wading boots.

Rushing into the bathroom, he washed up in a hurry. He pulled on his pants and shirt. Grabbing his socks and boots, he rushed down the stairs, right behind Uncle John. The smell of pancakes on the griddle was the perfect thing to finish waking him up.

"There you are. Eat 'em while they're hot," said Mom.

"Sure will," Ryan said, pulling on his socks and boots. He picked up his fork.

"Hurry up, and eat your pancakes," he said to his dad.

"No, Ryan, your father's not coming along this time," said Uncle John. "This fishing trip's just for you and me."

"But Dad always goes…"

"Not this time," said Uncle John. "Your dad has other important things to do today. Your fishing gear's already in my truck. I hear the trout are really running strong on the Gila River today. We don't want to miss out on that. Winking at Ryan's mom, he said, "We'll catch enough trout so we can all have a feast tonight."

Still puzzled, Ryan gobbled down his pancakes. When he was finished, he gave his face a quick once-over with his napkin, and was ready to go.

As they drove toward the river, Ryan told Uncle John about his wonderful dream. "…and I was on the podium, I was the champ, and holding my trophy high over my head. You woke me up before I could find out who finished second and third."

"Keep plugging away, and that dream can come true," said his uncle. "Anything worth doing is worth all the effort to make it happen, and you and your dad are certainly putting in plenty of that."

"Yeah," said Ryan, "I really don't know what I'd do without him. I'm sure lucky to have a father like him."

"Yes, you are," said Uncle John. "He's two years older than me, and he always looked after me when we were kids."

Ryan turned and looked at his uncle. "I never asked you before. When you and Dad were growing up, what did you two do for fun? Was there go-kart-ing then?"

'Well, yes, go-karting was started in the fifties, but the karts were created for grown-up men in those days. As we grew up years later, we made our own karts out of wood, used old discarded one-lung-er motorcycle engines, and raced on our country roads. We didn't have anything like the neat engine-powered go-karts you kids are racing today."

"No kidding? I thought everyone grew up with a kart like mine."

That brought out a hearty laugh from Uncle John. "Ryan, there are so many more things you kids have today than we did, but we still managed to have just as much fun. We used to go hiking, or play games in the woods, and ride our bicycles for miles until we came home so tired we could hardly eat our dinner. And then, of course, we had chores, just like you do, but ours were a different kind."

"Like what?"

"We grew up on a farm, as you know, so there were chores to do from morning 'til night. We had to help milk the cows and do lots of things before school. We also had to help work in the fields, tending crops after school, until dark.

"But," he added, "after chores, we had a great time jumping in the hay in the hayloft. Other times, we'd float down our creek on our home-made rafts, and swim with all our buddies until it got almost dark. Then Mom would call us home."

"Gee! That does sound like fun, but you certainly had a lot of work to do, too. I guess I'm glad I'm not being raised on a farm."

"It was okay, though. We also got to ride our horses when they weren't being used for farm work. Your dad and I used to try to out-race each other. That was our kind of horsepower – the real thing."

"Yeah, that does sound pretty great. I've never ridden a horse. All I know about horses is the horsepower in my kart. Dad's really sharp in teaching me how to work on it."

"He's a natural mechanic, and could fix anything he put his hands on when he was growing up. We once found an old abandoned motorcycle, and he had it running in no time, just by learning as he went."

"So that's how he gained all his skills."

'Yep," said Uncle John. "Your dad's a very smart man. I've always been glad to have him for an older brother."

As they drove, Ryan leaned back, closed his eyes, and pictured both of them galloping down a country road, laughing hard as they rode.

As they pulled up to the riverbank, there was already a large crowd of fishermen. "Looks like they had the same idea about fishing today," his uncle said. "We better hustle so we can catch our share."

Climbing out of the truck, they grabbed their gear. Walking downstream far away from the other fishermen, they found a perfect spot.

"Let's try this location first," said Uncle John. "We can cast our fishing lines from the bank. Sometimes the trout like to lie low for a while. Here's some bait for your hook. Made it early this morning. Used cheese in the mix; trout usually love it. If that doesn't get us enough of a catch, we'll put on our waders and try some red worms."

For the next hour, they fished mostly in silence, concentrating on every cast they made. The home-made bait was working. By ten o'clock their fishing creel was half full of good-sized rainbow trout. By noon, it was full, and time to head back home.

As they were driving home, Uncle John pulled over to the curb. He clicked off the engine and turned to Ryan. "And now, young man, I have some special news for you."

Another surprise? Uncle John was certainly full of them!

"I have something very important to tell you," he said, his voice much softer than usual. "It's about your father. You know that Silver Star medal that's been hanging above his dresser?"

"Yeah. It's been there for years."

"You knew your dad was in the Navy."

"Yeah, and he got that medal for something, but he never talks about it."

"There was a reason for that. Your dad was a Navy SEAL."

"I kinda knew that, but what *is* a Navy SEAL?"

"It stands for Sea, Air, and Land. Navy SEALs, Ryan, are the toughest and most combat-skilled members of the entire Navy, no doubt the most highly-trained men in our country's entire military. Their units are the strongest in the world. In the first stages of their training, it's so tough that seventy-five percent of the men drop out. But your dad never did. He went through every kind of staged military action, warfare training, and mission that the Navy SEAL Master Chief could throw at him."

"What's a Master Chief?"

"He's the most senior enlisted Petty Officer in the Navy. A Master Chief coordinates the training, and puts the men through the meanest, toughest assignments the Navy can come up with. Your dad and other SEALs went through all that to achieve the very special designation of Navy SEAL."

"Why did he do that?"

"Because he loves this country so very much, Ryan. You know him as your hero, but actually, he's a hero to this entire country. That's why he was awarded that Silver Star by the United States Navy."

Ryan listened eagerly for more.

"Your dad went on many extremely dangerous missions. And one was the most dangerous of all. That's why he has that permanent limp today."

"What happened? And why didn't Dad tell me this sooner?"

"I can tell you all this now, because that mission has just been Declassified."

"What does *that* mean?"

"That means that up until this week, his mission was such a dangerous one that it was kept a secret from everybody except a few people in the government. But now it's Declassified. And we can talk about it in public."

"So why isn't Dad telling me about this?"

"Because your dad's a very humble man, who never likes to talk about himself."

Ryan certainly knew that was true.

"So tell me about that mission."

"It was underwater demolition. He and his crew of Navy SEALs were extremely skilled in using SCUBA gear to work underwater. A secret message had come into SEAL headquarters. They were informed that a Navy ship in the harbor of Ramadan Bay had been rigged with explosives by the enemy.

"Those explosives were strung all along the bottom of the ship's hull. If that ship started its' engines, the vibration from them would blow up all the explosives, sinking the ship with all its' men to the bottom of the harbor." *That* had Ryan's complete attention.

"Go on..."

"The Master Chief knew your dad would be the best at defusing those bombs without exploding them, even underwater. The bombs were wired a certain way, and could only be disarmed by cutting a special red wire. So the Master Chief called for your dad -- and his fellow SEALs -- to take care of those bombs. His Master Chief would lead that mission."

Ryan was totally silent, his throat tightening, visualizing that terrible danger.

"No SEAL had ever done this exact type of mission before, so they strategically mapped out their plan before they went into the water. As they dived down deeper, moving quietly and very carefully, the water got darker and darker. The lights on their headbands could barely penetrate that murky darkness.

"They were determined to save that ship. The SEALs swam down towards the bottom of the ship's large hull. Finally, they could very carefully feel the location of the wires.

"Now they had to disable those bombs without blowing them up. The Master Chief, your dad, and the other SEALs worked together as they v-e-r-y gently clipped each fine red wire – barely able to see them with their headlights in the dark -- and disabled six bombs. They'd been told there were ten. Working slowly and carefully, with the proper air in their SCUBA tanks, the Master Chief and your dad each clipped another wire. Now eight bombs had been disabled. There were still two more to go..."

By now, Ryan's heart was beating fast, feeling intense fear for those SEALs...

"Suddenly, the Master Chief was caught in a booby trap, with razor-sharp wires, like prison wire, surrounding part of his body! He called out to the other SEALs on his radio. He was bleeding and in severe pain! If he could not get loose, he'd run out of air in his tank, and would not get safely back to the surface. Despite two more bombs to disable, your dad knew he also had to save his leader."

By now, Ryan could hardly breathe...

"He grabbed a special cutting tool from the holder at his waist, and managed to cut the injured Master Chief free from the vicious razor wire trap. With the other SEALs, he brought the Master Chief to the surface, rapidly turning him over to the SEALs who had already come up, who began medical aid…

"Then your dad turned back to disable the two remaining bombs. He soon found himself caught in a second razor-sharp wire trap. Like a bunch of extremely sharp knives, it cut completely through his knee muscles, and clear into the bone. The trap had badly severed those muscles, the water was red with blood, and your father was in excruciating pain."

Now there were hot, frightened tears forming in Ryan's eyes! His heart was pounding like a hammer in his chest! He could almost feel the sharp wires cutting into his *own* legs, as he listened. He could feel the intense pain -- and he could have lost his father -- forever!

Uncle John continued… "With his leg severely mangled and bleeding, your dad managed to cut himself free. Then following along the hull, he very carefully felt along the wires, and managed to disable those last two bombs.

"With only five minutes of air left in his tank, he brought himself to the surface. The other SEALs rushed him and the Master Chief to the Navy hospital, to take care of their severe wounds. But your dad and his group of SEALs had saved that ship and all its' men."

Choked with emotion, Ryan creaked out, "Is that how Dad got his limp?"

"Exactly," said Uncle John. "The razor-sharp wire had cut so deeply into his knee muscles and bone that even several surgeries in the Navy hospital could not restore them so he could walk normally again. But your dad was extremely proud that he and his fellow SEALs had successfully completed that dangerous mission. He said his injuries were a small price he paid to serve our country.

"*That's* why the Navy awarded him that Silver Star -- for his outstanding bravery. It's the third-highest honor in the Navy. He also got a framed citation. It's in his bottom dresser drawer. I know you're proud of your father, and now you can be even more proud."

Ryan felt more hot tears sting his eyes. His chest was heaving hard. "I'm sure thankful that he survived that mission!" he blurted out. Ryan had always considered himself a tough kid, but now he realized that his *father* was the really tough one in the family.

"While he was a SEAL, your dad went on many dangerous missions," said Uncle John, "and successfully completed every one of them. That's the reason he and your mom got so angry with you for shoving Kyle. They both know how much he suffered to keep peace in this wonderful country of ours."

As those words sank in with Ryan, Uncle John started his truck. "And now you know all about it. Let's go home and clean all these trout for dinner."

When they got home, Ryan gave his father the biggest high-five ever. He wanted to give him a hug, but felt that might embarrass such a brave and wonderful man. Having a dad like his, he felt like the luckiest kid in the world. Later, he slipped into his parents' bedroom, pulled out the citation, and read every word. It said:

CITATION

The Secretary of the Navy takes great pleasure in presenting the Silver Star to PO2 Cliff Edwards for exceptional valor in the face of enemy action. While removing explosive charges, placed by the enemy, from the hull of the USS John Winston, PO Edwards, though badly wounded by enemy booby traps, saved his superior, MCPO William James, who was also wounded, from certain drowning, at the risk of his own life. PO Edwards then continued on his mission to defuse the remaining explosives on the hull of the USS John Winston, successfully preventing the sinking and loss of all life on that vessel.

Carefully, Ryan placed the citation back in the drawer. Someday -- he and his father would hang it together.

CHAPTER NINE

Prepping for the next race, that weekend found Ryan and his dad back in the garage. After that last hard-fought Main, there was lots of cleanup on the kart. Again, they had made notes after that competition. Those helped them keep tabs on exactly how Ryan and his kart performed at every race, so they could improve.

What gearing did they use? Was the track "green" at the start of that event? Was the sun shining, was it cool and windy? How did the tires perform? Did they use new slicks, or older tires, in that race? How much air was in their tires during practice, qualifying, and the Main? Who finished first, second and third, so they would always know their toughest competition?

Not every team kept notes like they did, but that's exactly what professional race teams do. Since Ryan planned to be a pro someday, they did everything possible to help him succeed.

Ryan was looking forward to racing against Yoshida, who had now replaced Kyle as his biggest competition. He could hardly wait to get to the track, to see what he could do against his newest threat to the title. "There must be a flaw in him somewhere," he said to his dad. "I just have to find it."

"Okay," his dad responded. "I'll be your observer trackside, and see what I can discover, too." With those plans solidly in place, they loaded his kart and were soon on their way. Timmy had solemnly promised to behave himself if he could go back to the track, so he was riding in the backseat again. "Have you located that crim-nul yet that took our SCUBA tank?" Ryan asked him, a small smile on his face. But Timmy was still serious. "Nope, I'm still trying to find out who that was."

"When you do, be sure to let us know."

"You bet I will."

"And be sure that you stay out of trouble today at the track, don't be a jerk and go into the grids; just stay around the bleachers or on the hill, you hear?" Ryan did not want officials yelling at him again.

"I promise." Somehow, Ryan believed him.

More than ever, Ryan was ready to race. With *two* tough competitors – Kyle Sampson and Joe Yoshida -- he had to be at the top of his game.

As they arrived at the track, there was even more talk about the racing. Yoshida's competing had sparked new interest among the teams -- and the fans. The bleachers were almost full. The challenge was there. Ryan and his dad unloaded his kart. With no time to waste, they headed for tech. Again, no visible sign of Yoshida. They'd definitely meet on the track.

But his racing plans were abruptly changed. During his kart's inspection, Frank looked up at him, a puzzled frown on his face. "We can't pass you through, Ryan. Your clip's not securely fastened on your left rear wheel."

Ryan was in shock. He looked at his father, who was also surprised. "But, but, but...Dad and I worked on all of that, and everything was fine. Please check it again."

"I checked it completely, Ryan, and that clip is loose. I can't pass you through until it's fixed."

Ryan looked desperately at his dad.

"He's right, son. Let's take it back."

There was that crummy knot in his stomach again!

"Let's hurry," said his dad. "I'll grab the pliers, fix this, and you can still make it through tech before the first practice."

At their pit, his father searched for the pliers. He checked all around, but the pliers were not there. They needed them to fix the clip! What is going on?

First his SCUBA tank was missing. Now the pliers were gone!

"Ernie Farlow's pit's right next to ours," his dad yelled. "See if you can borrow some pliers so we can fix this right away!"

Ryan dashed over to Ernie. Quickly, he explained his problem. He soon had a pair of pliers. They tightened the clip, then checked the kart quickly from front to rear. As they worked, Ryan wondered: *Who was messing with them, and how did they do it?* Once they stopped work every night, the garage and truck were both locked. Definitely, someone did not want Ryan to win that title. They were doing all they could to prevent it!

They wheeled back to tech.

Frank began going over every detail. Ryan checked his watch. Time was flying by. Frank was taking a lot of time. Finally, he looked up. "Kart's okay this time. Go out there and have a good day racing!"

Now no time to waste. Ryan dressed into his safety gear as fast as he could. Then on to Grid B.

Practice was a tie between Sampson and Yoshida; they took turns grabbing the lead. Ryan was desperately running third. That clip problem had shaken his nerves. He almost did not get to race today! As he rounded the track, he breathed a "thanks" to Ernie Farlow. But where did his own pliers go?

"Oh, crap, I can't concentrate on that right now," he told himself. "Have to work on out-running these two guys!" Once his brain settled down with that thought, his speed began to pick up.

From the sidelines, his dad checked his stop-watch. By the fourth practice lap, Ryan had picked up a few tenths of a second. *That's the way to do it, Ryan,* his dad thought to himself.

Ryan was soon side-by-side with Yoshida, passed him clean, moved on to try to overtake Kyle. It was just practice, but Ryan wanted the wonderful feel of leaving Kyle in his dust.

On the sixth lap, he did it! Moving up near Kyle's kart, he carefully maneuvered around him, and took over the lead. Kyle shot him a frustrated hand move as he passed. "Hey, Kyle, it was a clean pass," Ryan muttered. "Tough, if you don't like it."

Back at his pit, his father logged his times in their book. Ryan had picked up those few tenths of a second. His kart was certainly running well. As he passed them on the way to the scale with his own kart, Kyle shot him another dirty look.

Ryan didn't even care. He did not have that hated knot in his stomach, either, for a change. Sometimes, giving a competitor their due makes all the difference in how a guy feels!

But deep down inside, Ryan wondered why Kyle hated him so much. Here was a kid who had every-thing – lots of money, the best equipment, and yet, somehow, he truly disliked Ryan, and made every effort to show it. How was Kyle managing to sabotage his kart? And why?

No time to worry about those questions. It was time for qualifying. This time, Yoshida outran everyone for the pole, with Ryan second, Kyle third, and again, Zane starting in fourth. Time to get down to work. Yoshida was a clean racer, but Ryan did not want an outsider ruining his chance at the title. Yoshida couldn't race for that prize, but he could sure stop anyone else from gaining valuable points if he kept running up front.

At the green, Yoshida shot away from the field, Ryan trying his best to catch up to that powerful kart. Yoshida led the first circuit. Ryan was closing in, but Kyle was also gaining on both of them. Despite his bad start, Zane began moving into the mix. All four of them were racing hard. With no effort, Yoshida still held the lead. Ryan kept trying to close in.

On Lap 6, Ryan was almost ready to make that pass. A slower driver was in his way. It was Farlow again, just cruising along on the track, enjoying his hobby, as he called it. "Hey, Ernie, you lent me your pliers, now don't mess up my racing!" Ryan shouted inside his helmet. As if he'd heard, Ernie signaled his move-over. Ryan sailed past.

It was a hard-fought battle all the way through. The crowd was on their feet, cheering and shouting at the excitement of a terrific race. White flag coming up! Ryan was ready to make a final pass on Yoshida, and take the lead to the checkered. Suddenly, he felt a bump! His kart began to skid out of control! He fought the wheel to keep control, but it spun out, shot up the small embankment, and flipped upside down! As he spun out, he got a brief glimpse of Kyle, shaking his fist as he passed to take second.

The red flag was thrown; the race stopped. Ryan wasn't moving. For him, *everything had gone black!*

Officials and corner workers rushed over to his kart, Ryan's father close behind.

"Are you okay?" yelled an official.

"I think so, but I can't see!" Ryan yelled back. Arrows of fear jabbed at his heart. "My eyes!! If I can't see, I can't race," he told himself, in panic. "And I -- can't -- see!"

Carefully, the officials lifted his kart and set it upright. Ryan still couldn't see; he was panic-stricken! Carefully, the paramedic removed Ryan's helmet from his head, where it had been jammed during the flip. Suddenly, a rush of bright sunlight flooded into his eyes! When his kart flipped, his helmet had somehow been forced down hard over his face, creating that frightening darkness.

"Oh, thank God, I can see again!" he shouted. "I'll be able to keep racing after all!" The fear flooded back out of his body.

Afterward, Ryan and his dad looked over the kart. It was damaged, but could probably be repaired. But when Ryan checked his helmet, his heart sank. In that flip, his helmet had scraped on the asphalt. His special American flag -- *and Rick Spears' autograph* -- were scraped so badly they could hardly be seen. That made Ryan so angry he was ready to punch Kyle out for sure this time!

The paramedic had checked him over. His body wasn't hurt, but there was a pain in his heart. Once a helmet's been in a crash, there may be hidden damage inside its' protective shell. This one would now have to be replaced. That would cost several hundred dollars! "I can earn another helmet," Ryan told himself, "but it won't have my American flag on it! What's even worse, a new one won't have that special Rick Spears autograph!" And yet, he was thankful that the helmet had done its' job. He had no head injuries.

"You're cleared to go," the medic had said. "Good thing you're in such good physical shape. That also helped save you from getting hurt in that flip."

That was true. To keep himself fit for his racing, Ryan worked at it. He worked out in his small basement gym, rode his bike everywhere with his buddies, made sure he ate the right foods.

Back at their pit, Ryan and his dad looked over the damage once more. The nose piece was cracked, all four tires were flat-spotted and ruined, there was other minor damage. "But considering the shape it's in," said his dad, "we should have it up and running before next month's event."

It would *have* to be ready by then. Today's accident had cost him more precious points! What's more, the thought boiled in Ryan's mind: *Kyle got away scot-free to finish his own racing today!*

Again, he'd done his dirty work just out of the sight of the officials, and lucky for him, the corner worker had looked the other way down the track just as he did his job on Ryan's kart. So again there were no witnesses, and Kyle went on race in the Main. *They call it "just hard racing," but this accident was unfair,* Ryan thought.

When Timmy saw the accident, he and Maria had come running down the hill. They were both relieved to know he was okay. "Maria, did you see what happened?" No, she hadn't. She was watching Arturo racing. Timmy wasn't sure, either.

"Rats!" Ryan said. "Didn't *anyone* see what Kyle did to cause that crash?" Sadly, he turned toward his truck. "C'mon, Timmy, climb on board. We'll have to watch the rest of the racing from here." Sure enough, Kyle won the Main, and scored more points! Yoshida finished second. Arturo had a good day, coming home fourth.

While they watched Kyle's victory from their truck, that knot in Ryan's stomach was really huge. "How can that guy keep getting away with what he does?" he said to his dad. "He has the greatest luck in town, that's for sure. I just wish I could find a way to get back at him!"

His dad turned the key in the ignition. "Don't even think about it, son. When we get home, let's check our inventory. Remember, we bought some extra parts with that kart. We probably have enough to get it running like new."

That would really be great, thought Ryan. As they drove toward home, he kept fuming to himself. "I sure wish there was some way I could prove what a dirty move Kyle made on me, but no one seems to have seen a thing! That really makes me angry. Kyle crashes me out, and no one can prove it, not even me. Sometimes I feel that life gets pretty unfair!"

Feeling his frustration, Ryan's dad let him ramble.

In the rear seat, Timmy was silent. He was usually a bundle of chatter, but he, too, was feeling really bad for Ryan, and had nothing to say to make him feel better. He'd been shooting pictures from up on the hill, but didn't think he'd seen exactly what happened.

As they pulled into the yard, Ryan's mom came rushing out the back door. "Are you okay, Ryan?" she asked, anxiety in her voice. "Dad called and said you'd been in an accident, but that you weren't hurt."

"I'm okay, Mom, but it sure was a crummy day," Ryan said. "First, the kart didn't make it through tech because a wire clip was loose -- and we had to borrow Ernie's pliers to fix it -- then I was racing really well until Kyle spun me out -- but worst of all, the

American flag and Spears' autograph on my helmet are completely ruined!"

Hearing his deep sadness, she said, "All those things can be taken care of, somehow. The main thing is that you aren't badly hurt."

Yeah, physically, he was okay, but that hurt in Ryan's heart was going to take some time to heal. The American flag could be re-painted on another new helmet, but he and his dad had no plans for another trip to the Indianapolis 500! There was no way he could get another Rick Spears autograph!

Feeling bad for his friend, Timmy gave him a friendly hug around the waist and headed off to his house to tell his folks what had happened.

Ryan and his dad again checked his kart. It didn't look too bad, but there might be hidden damage in the chassis.

"Tomorrow I'll call Ken at his race garage," said his dad, "and we'll have all the parts double-checked."

Ryan nodded. That was a great idea. Can't take any chances having a part break during a race. Once the kart was locked securely away in the garage, they headed toward the house.

Rushing out to meet them, Sparkplug ran around Ryan's legs, yipping and happy that he was back home. In the short time that Ryan had him, he and Sparkplug had become great pals. Seeing this busy bundle of fur jumping up to greet him made Ryan feel a lot better. It was good to have a dog for a pet again. Although his mom's Pink Lady rose bush was still struggling to grow, his mom was fussing less about Sparkplug. He was definitely a part of their family now. Later that evening, Ryan and his dad made plans for all the kart repairs.

CHAPTER TEN

After a cellphone call the next morning, they loaded up the kart and extra parts, and drove over to Ken's garage.

Ken also built go-karts. He was waiting for them. "Heard about your problem at Atlas yesterday," he said. "Sure glad that it was the kart, and not you, that got hurt."

"Yep, I am, too," said Ryan. "But we have to get it back in running order."

Ken was an expert mechanic; he had worked for a NASCAR race team. Carefully, he went over each replacement piece.

Holding his breath that no major problems would be found, Ryan watched silently as Ken next carefully examined every single part of the chassis.

Twenty minutes later, Ken declared the chassis was okay, and those extra body parts could replace any damaged ones.

That was great news for both Ryan and his dad.

"What's your bill for your work?" Ryan's dad asked, pulling out his wallet.

"Let's put it this way," Ken said. "When you're not racing, Ryan, or going to school, and doing other chores, why don't you come over one day and help me inventory some parts in my shop? That'll cover the cost of my work."

"Hey, Ken, that will be special! It's a deal!"

As they drove toward home, Ryan turned to his dad. "You know, yesterday, I felt like the entire world was against me, but people like Ken sure know how to make a kid feel better."

"Yep, just goes to prove that the world's not all bad, Ryan. Now let's get back to the house and tell Mom the great news."

Ryan could hardly wait. But as they drove in, his mom was in the yard, a strange look on her face. *Wonder what happened now?* shot through their minds.

She came hurrying up to the truck. "There's something here I want you both to see right now," she said, then hurrying around the corner of the garage toward the rose bushes.

"Oh, no!" Not again!" Ryan suspected it was Sparkplug. He'd been into her roses again! As he turned the corner, there she was, by her Pink Lady, pointing down to another fresh pile of dirt. The little wire fence around the bush was no longer standing up. It was crumpled over, and she was pointing to the bush.

"Darn you, Sparkplug! Why can't you learn to behave?" said Ryan, under his breath.

"Look at this," said his mom. "I tried to keep Sparkplug from digging there, but he wouldn't stop. He kept sniffing and digging, clear down to the roots."

They were both ready to scold the dog.

"I tried to push him away with a stick, but he just kept digging…and look what he found." She pointed to the open hole around the roots of the bush. "I don't understand this at all."

They both stooped down to see what she was pointing at. There was something shiny in the hole. Brushing aside a little more dirt, they both realized it was their missing pliers! And below them, a small wrench that disappeared sometime before that! They were both buried by the roots of the bush! How the heck did they ever get *there?*

Now they had another mystery on their hands! When they closed down the other night, they had laid those pliers on the rack below in the stand, and carefully locked the garage. The wire clip on his kart had been loose at the track, the pliers were gone from the rack, and now they show up *here*, along with a missing wrench, buried under his mom's prized rose bush!

Ryan dug out the tools, rubbed most of the dirt off them, and put them into his pocket. He'd finish cleaning them up later.

Now they knew it was not Sparkplug who'd been ruining her Pink Lady after all. It was someone burying those tools, and Sparkplug's keen nose had discovered them!

Again -- who? And -- why? And how could they get into the garage when it was securely locked? They still could not come up with that answer! Ryan felt Kyle Sampson had everything to do with it. But again -- how?

Quickly, he and his father checked the locks on the front and side garage doors. No sign of jimmying done there. No scratches -- absolutely nothing -- to prove they'd been tampered with. At this point, they had no explanation for anything.

Just then, Timmy came running up. "Wait 'til you see what I have!"

"Not right now, Timmy," Ryan said. They had much more important things to do than to deal with Timmy's latest discovery.

But he wouldn't be "shut down." "I took lots more pik-churs at the track yesterday, and I think you'll want to see 'em all. My dad showed me how to load 'em into his computer, and we printed 'em for you."

Reluctantly, Ryan took the photos. For Timmy being a new photographer, they looked pretty good. There were some of Ryan and his dad working on their kart, pushing it to tech, coming back with frustrated looks on their faces, fixing the wire clip. The photos were all sharp and clear – good camera for sure – and quite a good job of photography. As he leafed through them, Ryan saw some new racing action. Timmy had taken them from up on the hill, with his 300-millimeter telephoto lens.

There were shots of karts going through the hairpin, shots of passing -- very good – then something suddenly caught Ryan's eye! It was a series of photos – blown up large – of the action leading up to his spin, and the flip! Timmy's motor-drive had worked very well! *Now* Ryan could prove that Kyle tapped him hard and spun him out! *Now* he had the goods on Kyle, and could have him barred from go-kart racing -- *forever*!

But as he studied those photos more closely, he saw that – Kyle had raced him clean! It was a hard bump over a rumble strip that put Ryan into that flip! Kyle had taken the air off his kart, but had never actually touched him! That *was* just good hard racing on Kyle's part! It was all legal, and not a dirty deal after all!

Stunned, he handed the photos to his father. "Kyle did nothing wrong, Dad. He was just racing for position!"

Studying the photos, his dad was as puzzled as Ryan. "Then why would he continue to sabotage your kart?" Neither of them could come up with that answer. Also – how was he able to do his dirty work?

Ryan turned to Timmy and gave him a thumbs-up. "Great job with these photos. Do you mind if we keep them?"

"You kin have 'em," answered Timmy. "Thought you'd like to see how good I kin take pik-churs."

"You certainly can," said Ryan. "You certainly can."

Later that night, Ryan and his dad were busy with the repairs. They replaced the front spindle, put on four new rims and tires, checked over every part as it went on, and bolted on a new nose piece. While they worked, the same thought was going over and over through their minds. Exactly who was doing the skullduggery to Ryan's kart, and how?

They had gone over the entire inside of the garage for any signs of breaking in – plus the window, and again, the locks on both doors. Everything was clean; there was not a single sign of tampering anywhere.

When Ryan first got him, Sparkplug had barked and whoofed inside the garage those few times, but they had not thought much about it. *Perhaps they should have,* thought Ryan, and then they'd had to keep him indoors to preserve Mom's rosebush. If he'd been outside, would he have found an intruder? There were so many questions...

"It has to be Kyle," Ryan pondered. "He's the only one who tries to undermine me during the races, and calls my kart a scumbucket." But why, when Ryan had never had a harsh word with Kyle until that shove at the track? One question just seemed to pile on to another. *I'd sure like to go ballistic on him,* Ryan thought, *then maybe he'd let up on me.*

Finally, their work was done for that day, and it was time to lock up – again.

"From now on," said his dad, "we're going to keep a closer eye on this garage. And get an alarm installed to keep intruders out."

CHAPTER ELEVEN

L ater that evening, there was a knock on their kitchen door. It was Timmy again. "Just wanted to show you what my dad got me this time!" he said, smiling from ear to ear. He shoved a box toward Ryan. "Take a look! This is really neat! Now I kin be a real de-tek-tiv!"

Opening the box, Ryan looked puzzled. It looked like a simple pair of binoculars inside.

"With these, I kin check 'n see in the dark if anyone messes around again with your mom's rose bushes, or your garage," Timmy gushed. "C'mon outside and put 'em up to your eyes."

Not sure what to expect, Ryan did. He was amazed at what he saw. He could see the neighbor's cat, walking around in the darkness, clear as could be. It must have been at least forty feet away! "Now I kin be a real de-tek-tiv," said Timmy, punching the air. "I kin find all kinds of crim-nuls lurkin' 'round in the dark. My dad said I did such a good job takin' pik-churs that he wanted me to have this, too."

"Wow! That's pretty incredible, Timmy! I guess I'll have to behave after dark when I'm outside," Ryan joked.

"It ain't no joke, Ryan. These night vision bin-nok...bin-nok...oh, heck, night vision goggles... are a serious de-tek-tiv tool."

Ryan realized he had hurt Timmy's feelings. "You bet they are, Timmy, and someday you might be working for the FBI in Washington." He hoped that would make Timmy feel better, and it did. By the light from his kitchen, he saw Timmy's eyes light up.

"How didja know?"

"I was sure of it all the time," Ryan replied, holding back a chuckle.

"Ho, Timmy, come on home now." It was his dad, calling from their house next door. "Gotta go now," he said, and headed off into the darkness.

As Ryan went back to his house, he had a vision. Timmy was 25 years old, and was being awarded a special award by the FBI. "This is for your outstanding service to the FBI," the head agent was saying, as he pinned a special gold medal on Timmy's dark suit lapel, "for catching extremely dangerous crim-nuls."

Although it had been a really crummy week, Ryan suddenly burst out laughing. That really could happen someday. And he never explained that outburst to his dad.

Saturday dawned bright and sunny. All the repairs had been made to the kart, a new paint job applied. The number "03" had been carefully reapplied in the right places. Ken's Race Garage had ruled it race-worthy. Ryan was ready to go.

Again, Atlas Motorsports Park was alive with activity. The closer the racing got to the end of the season, the more everybody looked forward to the competition. Karts were being unloaded, engines tested, tech moved along rapidly, everyone seemed in a perfect mood. Ryan made up his mind that he wasn't going to concentrate on anything – just good solid racing, nothing more. He was going to keep his focus on that checkered flag all day.

Focus. Focus. Focus, Spears had said. No worries about Joe Yoshida, Kyle, Zane Ritchey, or anyone. He was going to run his own race, and hopefully, come out ahead in those points.

Timmy had tagged along again, and Ryan was glad. He was thankful that Timmy had documented the racing last time, showing that Kyle had actually raced him clean. That proved to Ryan that he shouldn't judge what he didn't know for sure. *No more jumping to conclusions*, he reminded himself. *Just concentrate on my racing...*

First practice went very well. They had set the proper gearing again for that track. Despite the accident, his rebuilt kart proved to be fine. He'd borrowed a Snell-approved helmet from another racer who couldn't make it that weekend. There were lots more lawns to mow, and his savings were growing. He would soon be able to buy his own helmet. And he'd be sure to have a new American flag and stars painted on it. Second practice went even better.

"Ryan, you're improving again every lap," said his dad. "I think your chances of winning this weekend are darn good."

And Ryan was definitely not planning to take it easy – no-sir! He was not going to rest on those fast times. Again he told himself – *Focus. Focus. Focus.*

It paid off in the Pre-Main. He was second fastest. Kyle, as usual, was first, Yoshida ran third fastest, Zane fourth. Kyle had the pole. That didn't mean he'd win the Main.

As the green flag waved in the Main, Kyle shot out to a strong lead, and Yoshida quickly passed Ryan.

Okay, he thought, *we're racing here. Let's show what you have!* Carefully maneuvering his kart through the hairpin, he found himself closing in just a little on Yoshida. But suddenly Zane shot past him, into third. There was a real dogfight going on among the four of them. *This is what I like – competition!* Ryan thought to himself. *Just let me at 'em!* But it was not as easy as he had hoped.

Kyle continued to hold his strong lead. Even Yoshida was having a hard time overtaking him. Zane kept dicing with Yoshida for second spot. Ryan was still playing catch-up with all three. But something was different today. Normally, he'd become angry, frustrated, and that stupid lump in his stomach would show up to aggravate him. Somehow, it wasn't there at all. He was truly enjoying his racing. Calm and ready to overtake Zane, he finally found his chance. Going into the tight hairpin, he poked his nose in again, slipped through on the inside, and now he was third!

Setting his sights on Yoshida, he watched Joe's line, following him through, again copying his every move. Sooner or later Yoshida would make a mistake, and bobble. Two more laps, Ryan was closing in! And there it was! Taking the outside lane up the banking, Yoshida left a small opening, Ryan gassed it, and powered past! Now he could take care of Kyle, who had it made up to now. Running in clean air, Kyle had kept a strong lead. Ryan tried his hardest, still couldn't catch him, and once again, Kyle beat him to the checkered!

"Rats! Kyle still leads the points," Ryan shouted inside his helmet. But then he mentally patted himself on the back. He was close to Kyle in points, and he'd also beaten Yoshida again!

After the weigh-in, his father was waiting for him back at their pit. "Some of your best racing yet," he told Ryan. "You're beginning to settle into some serious action. You should do just fine before the season ends."

There were only three more races left to win that title.

Just then, Timmy came running up. "I got some more racin' pik-churs of you," he said to Ryan. "I kin hardly wait to get home to show 'em to you!"

Ryan was getting to like Timmy more and more. Under Maria's guidance, he had learned how to behave himself. She didn't need to look after him anymore. He could go off by himself and not get into any trouble. Even the officials would smile at him as he snapped away at the racing.

Heading for home, Ryan and his dad recapped the day.

"You're getting better at picking just the right places to pass. That was a great move you put on Yoshida to gain second. Just keep on doing things like that."

"Yep," Ryan said, "but I still hate the idea of Kyle winning so much, and Yoshida gave me all I could handle today."

In the rear seat, Timmy had been unusually quiet again. Then he spoke. "Yep, that Yoshida guy's tough, but I have a secret. I'll tell you about it when we get home, and I know you're gonna like my pik-churs again."

Ryan smiled to himself. "Did you get a good shot of me making that pass on Yoshida?" he asked.

"Sure did, and I got some other ones that I know you're gonna like. I'll bring 'em over t'night."

"You do that," Ryan answered, "Dad and I can hardly wait to see what you got this time."

"Me, too," answered Timmy. He never said another word the rest of the way home.

Later that night, there was a knock on the kitchen door. It was Timmy. "Got your pik-churs now," he said, so excited he could hardly stand still.

"Boy, there must be some great ones," said Ryan.

"Yep, there certainly are. You're definitely gonna like 'em. And I did get that pass you made on Yoshida."

Proudly, he handed the photos to Ryan. "My dad says I'm gettin' better takin' pik-churs all the time. Been practicin,' you know."

Slowly, Ryan looked at each photo, then handed it to his dad. *These are good*, he thought. There was a neat shot of the four in a pack, challenging tight with each other. Another shot of Ryan passing Zane for third. And yes – there was that great photo of Ryan, making that pass around Yoshida to finish second. Again, the photos were sharp, and very clear. Ryan could easily read every detail on the karts. *By golly*, Ryan thought, *Timmy's learned how to "pan."*

Each time the karts had gone by, Timmy had his camera pre-focused. When the karts flew by on the racetrack, he moved the camera along with them, clicking his motor-drive as they moved across the camera lens. Timmy's dad had taught him well.

Ryan looked at them again, and noticed something else. In every other picture that had been taken of him racing before his accident, the American flag had been on his helmet. He felt a sharp tug at his heart. *I better mow some more lawns,* he thought, *so I can buy that replacement helmet soon.* He knew his dad would buy him one, but it wouldn't be quite the same. He felt he should earn his own.

"And here's the secret I toldja about..." Timmy handed Ryan a few more photos. Ryan looked at them, then looked at Timmy, a puzzled look on his face. "Where did you get these, Timmy?"

"I toldja. I took 'em."

"But these are pictures of a girl – with long, dark hair. Who is she?"

"That's the special secret. Joe Yoshida is... a girl."

Ryan almost dropped the photos. "C'mon, you're kidding me!"

"No, I ain't. I took those inside of Yoshida's truck. I'm tellin' you...Yoshida is a *girl*."

"But how did you take these?"

"It was right after the race. I was comin' back to your pit, Yoshida was walkin' back to their truck, and I thought I noticed a little bit of hair hangin' out from his helmet. It must have slipped out from his head-sock during the race. That got me to thinkin' -- most guys don't usually have long hair. So after he went inside, and waited to close the door, I stuck my camera in and snapped a few pik-churs before the door was closed, just to see what I'd get. She never knew I took 'em."

Ryan sat there in shock. "So all of us have been racing a girl, and even more surprising -- a *champ* who's a girl?"

There were lots of girls who raced go-karts, so why was this such a big secret?

"Heck, I don't know," Timmy answered. "But there must be some kinda reason."

"There *has* to be a special reason," Ryan's dad said. "I follow the Indy 500 and lots of other types of racing, including karting, and women have been in it now for some years.

"Janet Guthrie was the first woman to race in the Indianapolis 500, Lyn St. James was Rookie of the Year there in 1992, and raced there seven times, even set a speed record there of 225.72 miles per hour. Sarah Fisher raced go-karts and midgets starting when she was just five years old, like a lot of the young racers here at Atlas. In her early teens, Sarah won three WKA Grand National Championships, and she even became the first woman to co-own an IndyCar race team.

"Danica Patrick led in the Indianapolis 500 when she was a rookie in 2005, and finished fourth. She started *her* racing career in go-karts, won several regional and national WKA titles. Other women have raced in the Indy 500; many of them started in go-karting, so girls are pretty well accepted in karting. Yoshida's secretly being a girl is definitely a puzzle."

Ryan nodded in agreement at what his dad said. He made it a point that he would find out Yoshida's mystery...the next racing weekend. He could hardly wait. And he was sure glad that Timmy had been such a good "snoop."

CHAPTER TWELVE

It was soon time to go racing again. This time Ryan himself was going to play detective. His kart already through tech, he slipped discreetly over to Yoshida's truck. He paused for a minute. If he got inside, what would he say? And also, why did she go by the name of Joe? Was that part of the disguise? He meant her no harm, but wanted to clear up this strange mystery...

Finally, he knocked softly on the truck door. There was no answer. Again, he knocked, steadily, but gently.

He waited for a second. Still no response. Disappointed, Ryan turned to leave. Suddenly, the door opened just a crack, and the man who took care of her kart looked out. Ryan smiled.

"I-I-I'd like to come in and talk to Joe, please." The man looked startled. Apparently no one had ever asked that before. Ryan spoke again. "Can I come in and speak to Joe?"

The man paused, not sure what he should do. Motioning Ryan to wait, he disappeared from the door. Ryan stood, patiently hoping for some kind of response. Finally, the man came back. He beckoned for Ryan to come in. Stepping inside, Ryan saw Joe, sitting on one of the leather seats, wearing his -- her -- head sock.

Joe motioned Ryan to sit down. After a moment, he said, in a low voice, "Why do you want to see me?"

Ryan sat there for a minute, not sure what to say. Finally he got up the nerve. "I know your secret," he said, very softly, so he wouldn't upset her. "I know that you are a *girl*." Joe's eyes widened in alarm, her breath sucked in sharply. For a few uncomfortable moments, she never spoke.

Finally – "Why do you say that?" The voice was even lower now.

"Because I have pictures of you. I know my little friend should not have taken them, but he did." He handed her the photos. Carefully, she looked them over.

"And you believe him?"

"Yes, he's basically a good kid, wanting to be a detective someday."

There was a long silence. Then Joe spoke, and pulled off the balaclava. "Your friend is right. But now what do you plan to do with this information?" There was deep concern in her voice. "Ah...nothing," Ryan said. "I won't tell anyone your secret."

"*Are you sure?*"

"Yes, I'm positive. Unless you want me to, I won't tell any of the other racers -- or anyone -- that you're a girl." Joe gave a huge sigh of relief.

"But why do you pretend you're a boy?"

"It's a long story," Joe said "First of all, my father wanted to have a son. Instead, he got me. And my name? It's really Josephine, not a traditional Japanese name. But he has always called me Joe."

"That still doesn't explain your posing as a boy to race."

"That started a long time ago, when I was only seven. In our small town in Japan, there was a nice go-kart track, and we used to go and watch. I wanted badly to race, so my father bought me a kart. Yes, in most places in Japan, girls were gladly accepted in go-karting. But for some reason, in our town, girls were looked down on if they wanted to compete. When I first started, all kinds of bad things happened. I would be crashed out, sneakily nerf'd off the track so many times I lost count, my tires were even punctured.

"It was a very unusual situation. My father knew how badly I wanted to compete, and he saw that I did have talent. We studied the rulebook some more and found that racers could wear a head-sock. So that took care of everything. That's why I always wear my helmet, except when I'm here in the privacy of my truck.

"Father had always privately called me Joe anyway, so he signed me up again, under the name Joe Yoshida, instead of Josephine. Everyone thought I had a twin brother by that name, so I've been racing as Joe Yoshida ever since, even after we moved to the United States."

"And definitely winning, that's for sure. But... what do you do when your helmet is off and you're on the podium?"

"That's easy," she laughed. "I rush back to my truck, remove my helmet and balaclava, then quickly pin my hair up and tuck it under my cap. In this level of go-kart racing, there are no sponsors, so I don't have to change sponsor caps like upper-level teams."

Then she paused, still with great concern in her voice. "You said you would keep my secret. Now that you know the whole story, will you keep that promise?"

"You bet I will."

"And your friend who took these pictures? Will he be sure to keep my secret, too?"

"I'll get him to promise. Timmy's basically a good kid, and meant you no harm when he took those pictures. But there is one thing. Now that I know you're a girl, I promise I'll still race you as hard as ever."

She broke into a broad smile. "That's a deal, and you're on! Now we both better get down to business." She looked at her watch. "It's almost time for practice."

Carefully, so no one would see him leaving the truck, Ryan slipped out the door and went back to his pit. Taking his father and Timmy aside, he told them the entire story. They both promised never to spill the beans about Joe.

"See?" said Timmy. "I even put my hand over my heart just now when I promised." Ryan knew then that Joe's secret was definitely safe.

CHAPTER THIRTEEN

In practice, Kyle, Zane, Ryan, Yoshida, and Arturo tore around the track, feeling out the power of each other's karts. To no one's surprise, Kyle got the pole in the Pre-Main, with Joe on the inside pole, and Ryan third. "Boy, she wasn't kidding," said Ryan to himself. "She still means business!"

At the green, Kyle got off to his usual great start, but Joe began closing in on him right from the flag. She soon set him up for a pass. Kyle would have none of that, and quickly closed the door. Two seconds behind, Ryan watched them fight it out, down the long straight, up the slight banking, fast through the hairpin. Again, Joe set Kyle up with an inside pass through that hairpin. He cut across her lane and she slowed just a bit, to avoid a crash.

Let them keep fighting it out, Ryan thought. *They'll lose precious seconds; that will give me my chance.* Sure enough, on Lap 8, he saw his opening. He charged down the front straight, passing them both as they diced with each other. Joe finally won the battle over Kyle; she was now second. Racing up front, Ryan was in clean air, his engine pulsing with speed. Lap 9, time for the white flag!

It flew as he crossed the start-finish line. Slicing around the hairpin one last time, he headed for the front straight. He could see the flagman up ahead. Streaking across the stripe, he passed under the checkered flag. Ryan had finally won the Main again! It was a long time coming, and he was so proud!

That would definitely move him up in the points!

From the sidelines, his dad and Timmy were shouting, giving him a thumbs-up as he throttled down after his victory.

As they pulled into their driveway, the kitchen door flew open. His mother came rushing out! "Ryan, I heard that you won the Main again today! Your father was so pleased that he called me from the track!"

Even Sparkplug sensed that something was good. He was running around their truck in circles, barking as loud as he could. When Ryan climbed out of the truck, Sparkplug kept jumping up onto Ryan's legs. "So you know, too, huh, fella?" Ryan said, scooping his dog up in his arms.

After dinner, his mom said, "In all the excitement, I forgot to tell you. The alarm company called and said they are backed up. They won't be able to install the alarm on the garage until late next week."

"That's too bad," said his dad. "We'll just have to keep a sharper eye on things until then."

"Yeah," said Ryan. "I still can't figure out how Kyle's been getting into our garage. We'll really have to be on our toes. He was not happy at all that I beat him today. He may just try another dirty trick, even though we have my kart locked up tight as can be."

A half-hour later, their phone rang. Ryan's dad answered. It was Timmy. He was so excited he could hardly talk. "Hurry out to your garage! I just spotted someone sneakin' around it! I kin see him with my night vision goggles! Hurry before he gets away! My dad's puttin' on our outside lights so you kin see him better! *Hurry! Hurry!*"

Ryan's father shouted, "Let's go! Someone's messing around outside!" He shot out the door, Ryan right behind him.

Despite his limp, his dad was running as fast as he could go, chasing someone who was running away!

"I see his red hair!" Ryan shouted. "Stop, Kyle! We know it's you! Stop right now!"

The person kept running. Ryan's father caught up, and with one mighty leap, tackled him and brought him to the ground.

Sparkplug joined in on the action. He had bolted out of the house right behind them, and now was snarling and biting on the intruder's pant leg. Still squirming to get away, the intruder was locked in Mr. Edwards' tight grip and Sparkplug's strong teeth in his jeans.

Ryan shouted, "Okay, Kyle, No more dirty tricks from you! We caught you red-handed now!"

His father slightly released his grip, enough to roll the person over. "You're gonna pay for all your tampering!" Ryan shouted.

Then he looked at the intruder in the light shining from Timmy's house.

"What the...?"

The boy on the ground was not Kyle. It was Zane Ritchey!

"What the heck are *you* doing messin' around our garage?" Ryan shouted.

"Get your dog away from me! Get him away! Don't let him bite me!" Zane begged. "I'll tell you what you want to know!"

Reluctantly, Ryan reached down and pried Sparkplug loose from Zane's jeans.

Still holding Zane firm in his grip, Ryan's dad jerked him up to his feet. "Okay, now talk!" he told Zane, in a commanding voice. "Are you the one who's been getting into our garage? You the one who's been messing with Ryan's kart, and buried the tools?"

By this time, Timmy and his dad had rushed out of their house to help.

Ryan's mother, too, had hurried out to see what caused all the noise. They were all gathered around Mr. Edwards and Zane, waiting to see what he'd say.

Yeah, I did all those things," he confessed. "The SCUBA tank, too."

"But why did Kyle put you up to it?" Ryan shouted.

"He didn't!" shouted Zane, his eyes stark with fear. "Kyle doesn't know anything about all of this!"

"C'mon! Tell us the real truth!"

"That *is* the real truth! Kyle does not know *anything* about what I've done!"

"But then -- why? You did this to help him win because he's your friend?"

"No, he's not my friend, Ryan. I mean -- he is my friend, but the reason I did all this is because -- he's my *cousin!*"

So *that* was why Ryan thought it was Kyle who was tackled! He and Zane did resemble each other...

"But if Kyle didn't put you up to this, why did you do it?"

"It's kind of a long story," Zane answered. "Kyle acts mean toward you, Ryan, but he'd never actually do anything to hurt you."

Remembering all the close calls on the track, and Kyle's constant threats, Ryan found *that* really hard to believe.

"You see," Zane went on, "I did it because I wanted Kyle to win the championship. I thought that would make him happy."

"Happy?' Ryan burst out. "You wanted to make *him* happy? Here's a kid who can buy anything he wants -- except a championship -- he has rich parents, he has all the money he wants, the best of racing equipment, and you as a good friend – I mean, his cousin -- and you wanted him to win the championship to make *him* happy? Besides, what does that have to do with me? Arturo's a good racer, so is Randy Kennedy. You could have tampered with their go-karts. Why did you pick on me?"

"Because he's jealous of you…"

"Jealous of me? For gosh sakes, why???"

"Because you have everything that he doesn't!"

"What the heck is *that* supposed to mean?"

"Think about it, Ryan. You have a loving mom and dad, you have a great pet like Sparkplug, your father works together with you on your kart and works with you at the track…"

"So…?"

"Kyle doesn't have any of that…"

"Why not?"

"Because both his parents are gone! His dad was a wealthy executive. He was flying to a business conference, and Kyle's mom went along to keep him company. A sudden lightning storm came up, lightning struck the plane, and it crashed."

"Gosh, I'm sure sorry to hear that…"

"So who's the man who comes with you and him to the track?"

"Let me tell you the rest. The only close family member that Kyle had left was his dad's sister, Kyle's aunt. She too is very rich, but she's never been married, never had kids. She's always busy working with charities, and now here she was, left with a young kid to raise. It has not been a good combination."

"Why not?"

"Well, she resents the fact that she has to raise Kyle, and that takes her away from some of her charity work. It's great work that she does, but she had to leave some of her committees. She doesn't know anything about raising a young boy, so she hired Jim, who drives us to the track. He's a skilled mechanic, and does all the work on our karts. Kyle was still lonely, so because I'm his cousin, she bought me my kart and all the equipment so I can come to the track with him, too."

"But what about his school friends? Surely he has some fun with them…"

"That's just it! Since she doesn't know how to raise a young boy, she enrolled him in a private school in town. On weekends, all the other boys go home, so he has no friends on weekends, just me. Because he's in private school all week, he uses his spare time on weekends to practice and race. So other than karting, he doesn't have any real fun in his life."

"Again, I want to know – what does that have to do with *me*?"

"He's jealous of you because you have everything he doesn't have in his life!" Zane shouted, in exasperation. "*Don't you understand*? Let me give you an example... remember when you first got Sparkplug and he was barking at the window when you were eating your mom's cobbler in the kitchen?'

"Yeah..."

"Well, your dog was barking because I had ridden over to your house from mine on my bike, and was watching you and your family inside. I have a nice family. We don't have money, like Kyle, and mine are great parents, but Kyle feels that your family's outstanding. And that's why he resents you so much. He's a truly lonely kid. He may have a lot of money, but he does not have the love that you have with your folks. Heck, his aunt won't even let him have a stupid dog!"

Ryan was finally beginning to understand. The terrible anger that had festered inside him toward Kyle was slowly beginning to turn to sympathy.

"So tell us, then, how have you been getting into our garage?"

"Simple. One weekend when you were both at the track, you got busy with the kart, and didn't lock your truck. That was odd, because you always lock it. So when you were working on that, I slipped your keys out of the ignition, ran down the road to the key shop, and had them make me a set to your garage and your truck."

"So that's why we could never find a sign of tampering. You simply unlocked, and relocked, the door."

"Yep."

Another sudden thought flashed through Ryan's mind. "You realize then, Zane, that what you did to my kart was illegal. You were also breaking and entering, and we have to report all this to the karting association. That's going to kick you out of kart racing for good."

"Are you going to file police charges against me?"

"We'll think that one over, Zane," said Ryan's dad. "We realize you were trying to make things better for your cousin, but I think you're already beginning to understand what a stupid thing you've really done."

"If I wuz a de-tek-tiv already, I'd arrest him right now!" Timmy piped up.

Ryan's dad turned to Timmy. "Thanks for the outstanding job you did again tonight, young man, but you'll have to let us handle this one."

As Timmy and his father turned to leave, Ryan's dad loosened his grip on Zane.

"Okay, son, let's get your bike, we'll put it in our truck and take you home. Your parents will want to know exactly what you've done. And hand me those keys."

Reaching into his pocket, Zane handed them over.

As they drove through the streets, Zane said, "I'm guess I've really made a mess of things."

"You certainly did…"

"Will you explain everything to my parents – how I was only trying to help Kyle?"

"I'm sure we can do that."

"But will you let me do one more thing?"

"What's that?"

"Ryan and I are both off from school tomorrow, 'cause it's a teachers' conference in our district. Will you let me show you where Kyle lives?"

"I guess so, but why?"

"I just want you to see what a different world he lives in, and maybe you'll understand him better."

"I'm sure we can arrange that. We'll give you a call tomorrow." When they dropped Zane off, Ryan's dad told his parents the entire story. They were extremely upset, and sorry to hear about his actions. They offered money to make up for the troubles Zane caused, and said he would definitely be punished. Ryan and his dad declined the money; they said they just wanted to make sure it would never happen again.

As they drove back to their own home, Ryan was thinking...a lot. "You know, Dad, I guess we all take a lot of things for granted sometimes."

"Like what?"

"Well, just because Kyle had everything I wanted -- the finest kart, the best equipment, and everything -- at the same time he wanted everything that I have, two wonderful parents, a nice home life, good friends..."

"I think you're beginning to grow up fast, son. Those are real words of wisdom."

CHAPTER FOURTEEN

The next day, while Kyle was at school, Ryan, his father, and Zane headed for Kyle's house. They followed Zane's directions, passing through the business district, beginning to travel through neighborhoods with elaborate lawns and flowers. *Boy!* thought Ryan, *my mom would sure love to have some of these gardens. Look at all the flowers! And the roses!*

They drove up one hill, then another, until they were almost overlooking the city. Ryan had never ever seen it from up here before. Up one more hill, then they turned into a long driveway, flanked on each side with tall, beautiful trees. *This driveway must be 300 feet long*, Ryan thought. Finally, they arrived at a circular drive, in front of a large mansion. There was a unique marble fountain out front, with water splashing, and carved designs all around the rim. An ornate engraved door was at the main entrance.

"I called Aunt Ella and asked if we could come," said Zane. "She's waiting for us." He rang the bell.

Soon, a gentleman opened the door. "Hello, Zane," he said. "Glad to see you and your friends. Come in. I'll tell Miss Ella that you're here."

As they stood inside the front entrance, a woman appeared at the top of the foyer stairs. As she moved down the stairs, she almost seemed to float.

Ryan could see she was older, but still very pretty. And then he realized she had a very familiar face. She had been at the Rose Show, showing roses, too. So *that's* why Kyle was there, serving lemonade!

She invited them into a library/sitting room. "Zane's parents called and told me everything," she said. "I'm so glad that Kyle was not involved. Please let me know if there are any damages I owe you because of Zane, and I'll write a check."

"That's really not why we're here," said Ryan's dad. "We're here to see if there is something we can do for Kyle. Zane told us that he lost his parents."

She paused for a minute. "Yes, it was very sad. My brother and his wife were a remarkable pair."

"That's what Zane told us. We just wanted to meet you and let you know how sorry we are."

"That's very kind of you. I miss him and his wife very much, and it's a true challenge to raise a child when I never had one before."

"Again, let us know what we can do for you, and Kyle."

She held out her hand. "I appreciate that, but we are just fine." They chatted for a while, and then she said, "It was a pleasure to meet you, but now will you please excuse me? I have a board meeting at one o'clock today. Jared will serve you lunch before you leave."

On the way home, Ryan could now understand why Kyle was so lonely. Aunt Ella was very polite, but not friendly like his mother. In fact, Ryan felt that she too was a little lonely.

He began to plan what he could do for Kyle. Then he grinned. A few weeks ago, he was ready to punch Kyle out, and now he considered him a person who needed his help.

After telling his mother about Kyle's loneliness, she came up with a plan.

"Let's have Kyle and his aunt over for dinner, I'll fix them a nice steak dinner and my favorite pie. That might help."

Would they come? "I'll give them a call tomorrow."

When Kyle and Aunt Ella first arrived, their visit was uncomfortable and strained, but soon they were laughing and enjoying themselves. Turned out that Aunt Ella and Ryan's mom had more in common than he thought. They both had their favorite charities to help…and they both loved to compete with their Pink Lady roses.

And Ryan and Kyle?

"I want you to know, Ryan, how sorry I am for all my nasty actions toward you," Kyle told him, "and how much I appreciate being treated like a member of *your* family now." Ryan accepted his apology, and although it was tempting, he decided never to mention to Kyle about the lemonade spilled on the lady at the Rose Show. Instead, they talked about racing for the rest of the evening.

A couple days later, Ryan got a phone call. It was Zane.

"As you know, Ryan, I'm not allowed to race any more. I want to give you my kart, safety equipment, hydraulic lift, and helmet. You and I have the same head size. For sure I won't be needing them anymore."

Ryan held his breath for a second. Zane's kart was an Italian Tony Kart with a 50mm axle -- practically top of the line! His racing gear was, too! His helmet was a Snell-approved Bell. Jim was an ace mechanic; Ryan knew everything would technically be in great shape.

"I don't know what to say…"

"Please say you'll take them, Ryan. That's the least I can do after all the trouble I caused you and your dad."

Ryan said he'd talk to his father, and call him back later.

When Ryan's dad heard about Zane's offer, he let out a low whistle. "That's mighty competitive equipment, son. I think Zane's heart is in the right place now. Call him and tell him we'll be over to pick it up."

"I'll take it on one condition, Dad. Once it's mine, I gonna have it painted red, white, and blue. And the helmet, too, with an American flag and stars."

His father smiled and agreed. It was a perfect solution.

CHAPTER FIFTEEN

O n the final day of racing, Ryan didn't need his alarm clock. Neither did his dad. They were up bright and early, their equipment quickly loaded in the truck. As they pulled into Atlas, they could feel the extra excitement in the air. The stands were already crowded, the banners were snapping in the wind harder than ever, and everyone was paying close attention to each announcement coming from the tower.

In the rear seat, Timmy was again unusually quiet. Even he felt the tension of Ryan wanting to win. Since it was his last race of the season, Ryan's mother had also come along.

As they climbed out of their truck, a special announcement was blaring.

"Attention, all racers, family and friends! *Today is a very special event!* Not only is it the final race of the season for the championship, but Atlas Motorsports Park has a great announcement for all of you! When the championship trophy is presented today, it will be presented by a famous champion racer himself, who has flown across the country to do this special honor! *It is a huge privilege and honor to have this champion driver at Atlas Motorsports Park! The driver's presence will be revealed at the trophy presentation!*"

A huge roar of excitement surged through the crowd. Everyone was guessing who this special champion could be...

"Hey, Dad, that's really exciting!" Ryan said to his father. Instantly, the names of race champions were running through his mind. It must be someone who had won a national WKA or IKF championship!

He and his father quickly got their entry card, and pulled into their assigned pit.

Ryan was so anxious to compete that his heart was throbbing. His kart and helmet gleamed with their new paint jobs. Tech went smoothly for him this time. Transponders attached, he was soon on the track for practice. When the first Results Sheet went up, he knew today would be his biggest challenge. Kyle, as usual, was fastest, Joe was second, and he was third. He'd definitely have to pick up his times. Second practice – Kyle second, Ryan third, and Joe was in first!

In the Pre-Main, Joe swiftly took advantage of that lead, shooting ahead of the field and heading into Turn 1. Kyle was pressing hard; Ryan, too. Using her championship experience, Joe completely out-ran everyone on that first lap. Kyle moved in, pulling closer to her on Lap 2.

Ryan was determined. No gamble, no glory, he told himself, accelerating even harder. Pushing his new equipment to the limit, he gained on Kyle. Passing Kyle, he moved into second. Now he had to chase down Joe. Lap after lap, they swapped the lead. Toward the finish, it was still Joe out front. Fighting it out on the last lap, Ryan passed her just after the white flag flew. Working his way through slower traf-fic, Ryan took the checkered. He had the pole for the Main! It was Joe second, Kyle third, and Arturo was fourth.

This was what Ryan had been waiting for! On pole for the final Main of the season! As they lined up on the grid, he reached up and patted the American flag on his helmet. This race would be hard-fought, and he was definitely ready!

At the green, like Joe did in the Pre-Main, Ryan shot out ahead of the pack, setting up a strong lead. He charged into Turn 1, through Turns 2 and 3 and the next set of curves, heading for the hairpin. He was still in the lead, but Joe was beginning to close. Ryan neatly slipped through the hairpin, Joe close behind. Into the short straight, he gained more ground, and carved his way through the next hairpin turn. Maneuvering his way through the next four curves, he shot onto the front straight. Flooring the pedal, he made up more ground.

But he could hear Joe coming on strong. Racing hard through the second lap, she was now almost on his tail. By Lap 3, they were side-by-side; Ryan pulled ahead. Kyle closed in on Joe. Soon they were racing three-wide! With one swift move, Joe slipped into the lead! Ryan was second; Kyle on his tail. Constantly switching the lead, Ryan, Joe, and Kyle battled it out lap after lap. Then Kyle pulled ahead! For a while, it looked like he had a lock on the race, but Ryan shot back into first, Joe drafting into second behind him.

Again, another three-wide battle! Then Ryan charged ahead of Kyle on the inside of the hairpin, running up front again. The laps were rapidly winding down. Kyle and Joe caught up, and the three of them were soon in the mix of things again. It would be hard to find three more evenly-matched racers!

Slower traffic, including Ernie Farlow, was coming up. The three racers carefully made it through, passing all the karts "clean." Suddenly, the flagman threw the white flag, and the race for the checkered flag was on! They began fighting it out on that final lap, roaring into and out of the turns!

This is it! Ryan thought to himself. With Joe and Kyle once again on his tail, he charged as hard as he could. They caught up again, running three-wide, but Ryan powered back into the lead. They had only one corner left! Using all the power of his 125cc engine, Ryan shot across the finish line and took the checkered flag! He and Kyle had finished nose-to-tail! With braking problems, Joe had faded in those final seconds! With Ryan's victory, *the Jason Waldron trophy was his!*

As they stood on the Victory Circle podium, Ryan looked toward the bleachers. There in the front row were his mom and dad, waving and cheering at his success! Next to them, Timmy was busy taking photos of all three racers on the podium. Uncle John could not be there; he had important construction business out of town, but Ryan knew he was there in spirit.

Then he noticed the two people sitting next to his parents. One was Zane. The other was Kyle's Aunt Ella! Ryan reached over, nudged Kyle, and pointed him toward his aunt.

Seeing her for the first time, Kyle broke into a happy grin. She had finally accepted his racing!

Graciously, Ryan was happy that the others had also taken second and third. *Maria must be very proud of Arturo*, Ryan thought; *he scored a podium finish!*

Then suddenly a man holding the trophy climbed the stairs and walked toward him on the podium.

Ryan let out a huge gasp! It couldn't be, but it was – it was *Rick Spears*! What was he doing *here*?

Reaching out, Spears shook hands with a totally flabbergasted Ryan. Then he said, "With all your hard work and dedication, I knew you could do it, Ryan. Kyle's Aunt Ella reached me through the Indianapolis 500 office and told me about your damaged helmet," he explained, "so she flew me out here to be with you today. Let me see your new helmet."

Almost in shock, Ryan handed it to him. Spears took it and signed a new autograph. He handed it back to Ryan. It read, "Congratulations to Ryan, the Champ...Rick Spears." Then he said, "Keep up the karting, Ryan, even after you make it to the top in racing someday. It will always keep your racing skills sharp."

Boy, will I, Ryan thought. With gratitude in his heart to Aunt Ella, he eagerly pumped hands with Spears. When he and Spears came down from the podium, Ryan made sure he gave Aunt Ella a grateful big hug.

She hugged him back. "And you're all invited to dinner at my home tomorrow," she said to Ryan. "Mr. Spears will be coming to join us all. I want to know more about you, Mr. Spears, and all the karting, now that I've seen Kyle race. Please bring Timmy along, too."

Ryan looked over at Kyle. They exchanged grins with each other, then bumped fists together. Leaning toward Ryan, Kyle said, "I'm really glad that you won the title. I apologize again for all the trouble and nasty things I've said and done to you, and thanks for winning over my aunt."

"But that trouble's all over now," Ryan answered. "From now on, Kyle, we're buddies."

CHAPTER SIXTEEN

After the ceremony, Ryan, his mom and his dad went back to their pit, to load up everything and return home. Ryan's treasured trophy was carefully placed in a secure spot for the ride home.

"Hey, Dad, would you mind closing up our pit, while I take care of some unfinished business?"

"Sure, champ, you go right ahead."

Ryan headed over to Yoshida's truck. He gently rapped on the door. Her father opened it. "Can I come in?" Ryan asked. Her father nodded. Once inside, he went over to Joe.

"I heard about your brake problem in that final lap today," he said. "You were running one heck of a race until that happened. I just wanted you to know," he added, "that your secret's still safe with me. I also want you to know that if we both keep racing hard, hopefully, you and I will compete against each other in the Indianapolis 500 someday."

Joe broke into a smile. "Well, if you keep charging like you did today, I have no doubt of that. I'd love to take you on for a victory in the Indy 500." Laughing, they shook hands.

"Have to go now," he said. "Good luck. Hope to see you again next year at the next level."

"You won't be able to keep me away, that's for sure," she laughed. "I plan to keep you on your toes."

They both laughed again, Ryan said goodbye, and hurried back to his pit. Everything was ready to go.

On the way home, Timmy piped up. "I have all kinds of pik-churs of you racin,' Ryan, and of your ceremony, too. I even have pik-churs of Rick Spears signin' your helmet. I'll ask my dad to help me make an arrangement for your room."

Ryan settled back in relief. He had won the title and was presented the treasured Jason Waldron trophy by his racing hero, Rick Spears! He had won while his mom was there, been mightily challenged by a girl champion and beat her, and had now become friends with Kyle and Zane after all their wrangling during the season. Spears had said he was eager to talk to Ryan at Kyle's house the next day, to give him lots of racing tips. And he once again had his hero's autograph on his helmet! How good could life get?

But he and his dad still had some special things to do. Those would have to wait until they got home.

When they pulled up to the house, Sparkplug was there to greet them. Finally convinced that he was no longer the culprit ruining her roses, Ryan's mom allowed the dog in the yard by himself. Sparkplug was yipping and jumping up and down, happy that they were back.

Even his dog had played a special role in all Ryan's happiness. And so had Uncle John. Ryan planned to take his uncle out one day for a really special treat, in return for all his help, and also buy a special gift for Maria.

After he and his father stored his equipment safely away, they headed over to Timmy's. The alarm on their garage was now installed and set, although they didn't really feel they would need it nowadays.

Surprised, Timmy opened the door and invited them in.

Ryan handed him a large envelope.

"This is our thanks for solving all our mysteries," said Ryan's dad.

With curiosity, Timmy slowly opened the envelope. Inside it was money -- lots of it! When he took the money out of the envelope, Timmy was totally puzzled.

"Why are you givin' me *all this*?"

"Like we said," Mr. Edwards replied, "It's our thanks for solving all our important mysteries. We didn't need Ryan's other go-kart, so we sold it. That money is yours. Now you and your father can buy that Cadet kart that you've been wanting so badly."

"Wowie, Dad and Mom, come in here!" yelled Timmy, leaping high into the air. "Look at what Ryan and his dad have done for me!"

His parents rushed into the room, and Timmy was so excited that he just babbled, so Ryan's dad quickly explained their gift to Timmy's parents.

"Timmy's a darn good kid,' Ryan added. "We appreciated all his great help. And we'll help him with his racing." When the excitement with Timmy and his parents finally died down, Ryan and his dad headed back home.

He and his parents now had two final things to complete. Laughing as the three of them went upstairs arm-and-arm with Sparkplug leading the way, they knew exactly what they planned to do.

First they went into his mom and dad's bedroom. Opening the bottom drawer on his dad's dresser, Ryan took out the framed Silver Star citation. Quickly, as his parents watched, Ryan hammered into the wall a hook he had specially saved in that room. He handed the citation to his dad.

Then he and his mother proudly stood back as his father hung it on the wall, right next to the Silver Star medal. Ryan gave his dad a respectful military salute; he was now an even greater hero to Ryan.

There was still one more important thing left. There was that open spot reserved on Ryan's trophy shelf in his bedroom. He and his parents carried in the cherished Waldron championship trophy. Together, they placed it into that special treasured spot, and stepped back to admire it.

Standing up tall on his hind legs, Sparkplug put his paws on the shelf and gave it his own bark of approval.

Now, Ryan felt, life was perfect. And the Indianapolis 500 -- and the Borg-Warner trophy -- were somewhere ahead down the road...

He had already kissed those famous bricks at Indy's start/finish line, and was looking forward to the next time he planned to kiss them -- as an Indianapolis 500 champion!

-END-

"In this book, the go-karting explains the sport well. It also provides a great example for young boys and girls about preparation, hard work, sportsmanship, friendship, integrity, family, and other life lessons. Lots of suspense, and the story of Joe caught me completely off-guard; it really adds to the story. I'm happy to give this book my 'thumbs up.' Well-done!"

— Lyn St. James, 1992 Indy 500 Rookie of the Year

"At seven, I got my first ride at Pepe's Go-Kart Land, and the freedom and exhilaration on that first lap was unforgettable! Today I earn my living driving 300 miles per hour in the world of nitro drag racing. Kay Presto has utilized her amazing talent to create this novel about go-kart racing that is compelling, yet easy to read. This book should motivate every child to read, and find their passion. I can't wait to find out how many of them will one day make a living behind the racing steering wheel!"

— Jack Beckman, 2003 NHRA Super Comp Champion, and record-setting 2012 NHRA Nitro Funny Car World Champion

"I'm happy to see someone address youth kart racing in a fun and positive way!"

— Bob Bondurant, Founder/Owner of Bob Bondurant's School of High-Performance Driving and Go-Karting

"This book gave me a birds-eye view of my life when I was go-karting as a kid; it made me think back on how valuable those challenging experiences were. This book shows the meaning of hard work through the good and bad; things won't always be given to you and you have to work for what you want. In the end, Ryan experienced that what you receive in pursuing your dream builds not only a relationship with your family, but an education in life. Loved the mystery and twists and turns throughout the entire book; kept me guessing to the end. Great read!"

— Kenton Koch, 2016 Rolex Daytona 24-Hour Winner

ABOUT THE AUTHOR

Kay Presto has covered motor-sports of all types for over four decades. She has received numerous national awards for her motorsports coverage on international television and radio, also in journalism and photography for international magazines and coffee-table books. She has done public relations for race teams, and currently has her own motorsports website -- www.carsandcompetition.com.

She's the co-author and photographer for the award-winning book *Power Basics of Auto Racing* -- written for high-school students -- and co-producer of the video of the same name. Her true-life stories are published in various Chicken Soup and Heart Series books. She loves writing for children, and currently is the author of twelve other children's books. She's a noted speaker at conventions and other major events.

Presto lives in California. You can visit her online at KayPrestoauthor.wordpress.com

Special note:

This book is a tribute to the *real four-time winner of the Indianapolis 500* – Rick Mears.